Mastering TESOL

Mastering TESOL

A Comprehensive Guide to Teaching English to Speakers of Other Languages

Amir Abbas Ravaei

Success Publications Sar

Copyright © 2024 by Amir Abbas Ravaei

All rights reserved. No part of this book may be reproduced in any manner whatsoever without written permission except in the case of brief quotations embodied in critical articles and reviews.

First Printing, 2024

CONTENTS

1-1

What is TESOL?

1-2

The Importance of English as a Global Language

1-3

The Roles of a TESOL Teacher

1-4

Historical Overview of TESOL

Chapter 2 | Teachers and Learners   24

CONTENTS

1 | Mastering TESOL: A Comprehensive Guide to Teaching English to Speakers of Other Languages   1

2 | About This Book   2

3 | About the Author   3

4 | Acknowledgement   4

Cahpter 1 | Introduction to TESOL   5

CONTENTS

2-1

Characteristics of a good teacher

2-2

What makes a good learner?

2-3

What Should I Know About My ESL Students?

2-4

Why do adults learn English?

2-5

Differences every teacher should know about Adults and Children

2-6

English language levels

Chapter 3 | English Language Teaching Methodology   48

CONTENTS

3-1
English Language Methodology: A Comprehensive Exploration

3-2
The Grammar-Translation Method: An In-Depth Exploration

3-3
The Audio-Lingual Method: A Comprehensive Overview

3-4
A Comprehensive Guide to the Presentation, Practice, and Production (PPP) Method for Language Teaching

3-5
The Task-based Method: Exploring Key Concepts, Components, and Applications

3-6
Communicative Language Teaching: A Comprehensive Overview

3-7
Embracing the Power of the Community Language Learning Method

3-8
Community Language Learning

CONTENTS

3-9

The Silent Way

3-10

Suggestopaedia

3-11

The Lexical Approach

3-12

Engage, Study and Activate

Chapter 4 | Classroom Management 107

CONTENTS

4-1

Classroom Management

4-2

Harnessing the Power of Eye Contact in the English Teaching Classroom

4-3

The Power of Gestures in the Classroom

4-4

Harnessing the Power of the Teacher's Voice in the English Teaching Classroom

4-5

Why should we use Students' Names in an English Language Class?

4-6

Grouping Students in English Language Classes: Advantages and Disadvantages

4-7

Exploring the Advantages and Disadvantages of Pair Work in English Language Classes

4-8

Exploring Effective Seating Arrangements in the English Language Classroom

CONTENTS

4-9

The Importance of Teacher's Sitting and Standing Positions in an English Language Class

4-10

Balancing Teacher Talking Time and Student Talking Time in English Language Classes

4-11

Establishing Rapport

4-12

Problem Behavior in English Language Classes: Causes, Impacts, and Strategies for Effective Classroom Management

Chapter 5 | Presenting and Practicing Language 157

CONTENTS

5-1

Understanding English Vocabulary

5-2

A Sample Lesson Plan for Teaching Vocabulary

5-3

English Language Functions

5-4

Why is it important to teach English Language Functions?

5-5

Lesson Plan: Teaching English Functions - Giving Directions

Chapter 6 | Teaching Skills and Techniques 178

CONTENTS

6-1

Teaching Listening

6-2

Teaching Speaking

6-3

Teaching Reading

6-4

Teaching Writing

6-5

Error Correction

6-6

Techniques for Correcting Writing Assignments

Chapter 7 | Linguistics for TESOL 205

7-1
Morphology

7-2
Syntax

7-3
Semantics

7-4
Pragmatics

7-5
Teaching Pronunciation and Phonology

7-6
Stress and Intonation

Chapter 8 | Lesson Planning 234

8-1
Lesson Planning

Chapter 9 | Course Materials 241

9-1
Effective Use of Materials in the Classroom

Chapter 10 | Assessment and Testing 247

CONTENTS

10-1
Formative and Summative Assessments

10-2
Rubrics and Assessment

10-3
Feedback and Grading

Chapter 11 | Specialized TESOL Contexts 259

11-1
Teaching Business English

11-2
Teaching Academic English

11-3
Teaching English for Specific Purposes (ESP)

11-4
Teaching English to Young Learners

11-5
Teaching English on a One-on-One Basis

Mastering TESOL: A Comprehensive Guide to Teaching English to Speakers of Other Languages

About This Book

"Mastering TESOL: A Comprehensive Guide to Teaching English to Speakers of Other Languages" provides a thorough exploration of the TESOL field, equipping both novice and experienced teachers with the knowledge and tools needed to excel in English language education. Whether you're a teacher in a traditional classroom setting or an online instructor working with learners from diverse backgrounds, this book serves as an invaluable resource on your journey to becoming an effective TESOL professional.

About the Author

Amir Abbas Ravaei holds a PhD in TESOL and is the founder and CEO of the Vancouver TESOL Training Center in North Vancouver, Canada. He is a Teacher Trainer and Consumer Choice Awards winner for the best language school in Greater Vancouver.

He is also the National Director of the T.I.E.L.C Regional Board of TESOL Authority.

Acknowledgement

I would like to express my deepest gratitude and appreciation to all individuals who have contributed to the successful completion of this book. Firstly, I would like to thank my family who have been my unwavering support system throughout this journey. Their constant encouragement, love and understanding have been instrumental in making this possible. I am also grateful to my friends and colleagues who have offered their valuable insights and feedback, helping me to refine my ideas and shape the content of this book. I would like to extend my heartfelt thanks to my editor, who has provided guidance and expert advice in the writing process. Their knowledge and expertise in the field have been invaluable. Finally, I would like to thank my publisher, who has believed in this project and provided the necessary resources and support to bring this book to fruition. Thank you all for your invaluable contributions and unwavering support. This book would not have been possible without your help.

Cahpter 1

Introduction to TESOL

1-1

What is TESOL?

Teaching English to Speakers of Other Languages, often abbreviated as TESOL, is a dynamic and globally recognized field that encompasses various methods, approaches, and strategies for teaching the English language to non-native speakers. As the world becomes increasingly interconnected, the demand for English language proficiency has skyrocketed, making TESOL an essential discipline in education and language development. In this comprehensive article, we will delve deep into the world of TESOL, exploring its history, significance, methodologies, and the opportunities it offers to both educators and language learners.

1. **What is TESOL?**

    TESOL, an acronym for Teaching English to Speakers of Other Languages, is an umbrella term that encompasses a range of practices and methodologies aimed at teaching English to individuals whose first language is not English. It is a multifaceted field that includes English as a Second Language (ESL) and English as a Foreign Language (EFL) instruction, as well as variations such as English for Specific Purposes (ESP) and English for Academic Purposes (EAP). TESOL professionals work with students of all ages, from young learners to adults, in diverse educational settings worldwide.

2. **Historical Evolution of TESOL**

   The roots of TESOL can be traced back to the late 19th century when English-speaking missionaries began teaching English to non-native speakers. However, it wasn't until the mid-20th century that TESOL as a formal discipline began to take shape. One of the most significant developments was the advent of the audio-lingual method, which gained popularity during World War II as a means of quickly teaching military personnel to communicate in foreign languages. This method focused on repetition and mimicry and heavily influenced early TESOL practices.

   The 1960s and 1970s witnessed a shift towards more communicative approaches to language teaching, driven by linguists and educators like Noam Chomsky and Stephen Krashen. These theories highlighted the importance of meaningful communication and understanding the underlying structures of language. This shift marked the beginning of a more learner-centered and communicative approach to TESOL.

   Today, TESOL has evolved into a diverse field that draws from various educational philosophies and methods, including communicative language teaching, task-based learning, and content-based instruction, among others.

3. **The Significance of TESOL**

   TESOL plays a crucial role in today's globalized world for several reasons:

   a. Economic Opportunities: English proficiency is often a prerequisite for employment in various sectors, from business to tourism. TESOL equips individuals with the language skills needed to access these economic opportunities.

   b. Academic Advancement: English is the language of instruction in many international universities and academic programs.

TESOL prepares students to excel in these contexts.

c. Cross-Cultural Communication: As people from diverse linguistic backgrounds interact more frequently, TESOL fosters effective communication, understanding, and cultural exchange.

d. Empowerment and Integration: TESOL helps immigrants and refugees integrate into new societies and participate fully in educational and social activities.

4. **Methodologies and Approaches in TESOL**

TESOL employs various teaching methodologies and approaches tailored to the needs of learners and the context of instruction. Some of the prominent methods and approaches include:

a. Communicative Language Teaching (CLT): Emphasizes communication and interaction as the primary goals of language learning. Learners engage in real-life situations to develop practical language skills.

b. Task-Based Language Teaching (TBLT): Focuses on language learning through the completion of meaningful tasks, which encourages problem-solving and language acquisition simultaneously.

c. Content-Based Instruction (CBI): Integrates language learning with content from other subjects (e.g., science, history), enabling students to acquire language while learning about specific topics.

d. The Direct Method: Advocates teaching a second language without the use of the student's native language. This method relies on immersion and visual aids.

e. The Grammar-Translation Method: Emphasizes the study of grammar rules and translation of texts. It is less focused on spoken communication.

f. The Audio-Lingual Method: Emphasizes repetition and pattern drilling to develop speaking and listening skills.

5. **Professional Development in TESOL**

   Becoming a qualified TESOL professional typically involves obtaining a TESOL certification or a related qualification, such as a Teaching English as a Foreign Language (TEFL) or a Teaching English as a Second Language (TESL) certificate. These programs provide in-depth training on language teaching methodologies, classroom management, and assessment techniques.

   For those interested in pursuing a career in TESOL, there are various pathways, including:

   a. Bachelor's and Master's Degrees: Many universities offer undergraduate and graduate programs in TESOL or related fields like Applied Linguistics.

   b. Online TESOL Certification: Online courses provide flexible options for individuals looking to become certified TESOL instructors.

   c. On-Site TESOL Training: Some programs offer intensive on-site training, which can be especially valuable for gaining practical teaching experience.

   d. Professional Associations: Joining organizations like TESOL International Association provides access to resources, networking opportunities, and conferences that enhance professional development.

6. **TESOL in Practice**

   TESOL professionals work in diverse settings, including public and private schools, language institutes, universities, and corporate training centers. They cater to a wide range of learners, from young children learning the basics of English to adults aiming to improve their business communication skills. Additionally, TESOL instructors may find themselves teaching in various countries, embracing new cultures, and experiencing unique challenges and rewards.

7. Challenges and Future Directions

TESOL faces several challenges, including the need to continually adapt to changing technology, the demand for English in specific professional contexts (e.g., aviation, healthcare), and the ongoing debate on the most effective teaching methods. Moreover, the role of English as a global lingua franca raises questions about the preservation of cultural and linguistic diversity.

In the future, TESOL is likely to evolve in response to these challenges. Technology will play an increasingly significant role, with the integration of AI and online platforms offering new opportunities for language learning. TESOL professionals will need to stay abreast of these developments to provide effective instruction.

TESOL, or Teaching English to Speakers of Other Languages, is a dynamic and essential field that empowers individuals with the language skills needed to thrive in a globalized world. From its historical origins to its diverse methodologies and significant impact, TESOL continues to shape the way English is taught and learned worldwide. As we look to the future, TESOL will remain at the forefront of language education, adapting to new challenges and opportunities in our interconnected world.

The Importance of English as a Global Language

English is often referred to as the global lingua franca, and its importance as a global language cannot be overstated. It plays a pivotal role in various aspects of our interconnected world, and here are some reasons highlighting its significance:

1. **Communication:** English serves as a common means of communication among people from diverse linguistic backgrounds. Whether it's in business, diplomacy, academia, or travel, English bridges language barriers and enables effective communication.

2. **Economic Opportunities:** English proficiency is a valuable skill in the global job market. Many multinational companies and organizations conduct their business in English, and a command of the language can significantly enhance one's career prospects.

3. **Education:** A substantial portion of academic content, especially in higher education, is available in English. Many prestigious

universities and research institutions around the world use English as the primary language of instruction and publication. This facilitates knowledge exchange and international collaboration.

4. **Science and Technology:** English is the predominant language in the fields of science and technology. Researchers and scientists from different countries use English to share their findings, contributing to the rapid advancement of these fields.

5. **Cultural Exchange:** English-language literature, movies, music, and media have a global reach. Understanding English allows individuals to access and appreciate a wide range of cultural content from different parts of the world.

6. **Diplomacy and International Relations:** English is commonly used in international diplomacy and negotiations. It facilitates cooperation and understanding among nations, as diplomats and representatives can communicate effectively in a common language.

7. **Tourism:** English is the most widely spoken language in the tourism industry. Travellers often find it helpful to have at least a basic understanding of English when visiting foreign countries.

8. **Internet and Information Access:** A significant portion of online content is in English. English proficiency makes it easier to access information, engage in online discussions, and participate in global conversations on various platforms.

9. **Globalization:** English has become a symbol of globalization. As the world becomes more interconnected economically, socially, and culturally, English serves as a unifying force that brings people together.

10. **Soft Power:** English-speaking countries, such as the United States and the United Kingdom, often have a strong cultural and political influence on the global stage. Their media, entertainment, and values are disseminated through the English language.

11. **Innovation and Business:** Many breakthroughs in technology and innovation emerge from English-speaking regions. To stay current in these fields and participate in global business networks, proficiency in English is essential.

In conclusion, English has become the global language of communication, facilitating interactions across borders and cultures. Its importance in the modern world is undeniable, as it enables people to access opportunities, share knowledge, and connect with others on a global scale.

1-3

The Roles of a TESOL Teacher

A TESOL (Teaching English to Speakers of Other Languages) teacher plays several important roles in the language learning process for non-native English speakers. These roles go beyond just teaching grammar and vocabulary; they encompass various aspects of language acquisition and cultural understanding. Here are some of the key roles of a TESOL teacher:

1. **Language Instructor:** The primary role of a TESOL teacher is to teach English language skills, including speaking, listening, reading, and writing. They help students develop their language proficiency through structured lessons and activities.

2. **Facilitator:** TESOL teachers facilitate the learning process by creating a supportive and engaging classroom environment. They encourage active participation, discussions, and collaboration among students.

3. **Curriculum Designer:** TESOL teachers design and adapt curriculum materials to meet the needs and proficiency levels of their

students. They often create lesson plans, select textbooks, and choose teaching resources.

4. **Assessor and Evaluator:** TESOL teachers assess their students' language proficiency through various methods, such as quizzes, tests, assignments, and spoken assessments. They use this information to track progress and provide feedback.

5. **Cultural Ambassador:** TESOL teachers often introduce students to the cultural aspects of English-speaking countries. This includes customs, traditions, idiomatic expressions, and social norms, helping students understand the context in which the language is used.

6. **Motivator and Encourager:** TESOL teachers play a crucial role in motivating and encouraging students to persist in their language learning journey. They provide positive reinforcement and support to boost students' confidence.

7. **Problem Solver:** TESOL teachers need to address various challenges that students may encounter in their language learning process, such as pronunciation difficulties, grammar confusion, and language barriers.

8. **Cross-Cultural Communicator:** TESOL teachers facilitate communication between students from diverse cultural backgrounds. They help students bridge cultural gaps and develop intercultural communication skills.

9. **Classroom Manager:** TESOL teachers are responsible for maintaining discipline and managing the classroom effectively. This includes setting rules, establishing routines, and handling behavioral issues when they arise.

10. **Resource Provider:** TESOL teachers often recommend and provide additional resources, such as online language learning tools, books, and multimedia materials, to help students practice English outside the classroom.

11. **Professional Development:** Continuous learning is crucial in the field of TESOL. TESOL teachers should engage in professional development to stay updated with the latest teaching methodologies and language acquisition research.

12. **Advocate for Students:** TESOL teachers advocate for their students' language needs and may provide guidance on language proficiency exams, college applications, or career opportunities where English proficiency is essential.

In summary, a TESOL teacher's role goes beyond traditional teaching; it involves guiding students in their language learning journey, fostering cultural understanding, and helping students become effective communicators in English-speaking contexts.

1-4

Historical Overview of TESOL

Teaching English to Speakers of Other Languages (TESOL) is a field of education that has evolved over the years to meet the growing demand for English language instruction around the world. Here's a historical overview of TESOL:

1. **Early Beginnings (19th Century):**
     - The roots of TESOL can be traced back to the 19th century when British and American missionaries and colonial administrators began teaching English to non-native speakers in various parts of the world.

2. **Rise of the British Council (1930s):**
     - The British Council played a significant role in the development of TESOL. In the 1930s, it began offering English language courses and teacher training programs in various countries, contributing to the spread of English language teaching.

3. **World War II and Post-War Era:**

- The need for English language instruction increased during and after World War II due to military and diplomatic interactions. The British Council and the American government played a crucial role in establishing English language programs for soldiers and diplomats.

4. **Emergence of TESOL as a Discipline (1960s-1970s):**
    - The 1960s and 1970s saw the formalization of TESOL as a distinct discipline. Organizations like TESOL International Association (formerly Teachers of English to Speakers of Other Languages) were founded during this period to promote research and professional development in the field.

5. **Communicative Language Teaching (CLT):**
    - In the 1970s and 1980s, Communicative Language Teaching (CLT) gained prominence. CLT emphasized the importance of teaching language for real communication and interaction, rather than just rote memorization of grammar rules.

6. **Technology and Distance Learning (Late 20th Century):**
    - Advances in technology, particularly the development of the internet, transformed TESOL. Online resources, computer-assisted language learning (CALL), and distance education became integral to language instruction.

7. **English as a Global Language:**
    - The late 20th and early 21st centuries witnessed the rapid spread of English as a global lingua franca. This led to

increased demand for English language instruction in diverse contexts, including business, academia, and tourism.

8. **Focus on Standards and Assessment:**
    - Standards for language proficiency assessment, such as the Common European Framework of Reference (CEFR) and the Test of English as a Foreign Language (TOEFL), became important in the TESOL field, providing a common framework for measuring language proficiency.

9. **Diversity in TESOL (21st Century):**
    - TESOL has evolved to embrace diversity in terms of learner needs and contexts. It includes English for Specific Purposes (ESP), English for Academic Purposes (EAP), English for Business, and more specialized areas of language instruction.

10. **Continuing Evolution:**
    - TESOL continues to evolve in response to changing demographics, technological advances, and pedagogical research. The field remains dynamic and adaptable to the evolving needs of English language learners worldwide.

In summary, TESOL has a rich history that reflects the changing global landscape and the growing importance of English as a global language. It has evolved from its early missionary and colonial roots to become a well-established field with a focus on effective language teaching methodologies and assessment practices.

Chapter 2

Teachers and Learners

2-1

Characteristics of a good teacher

A good teacher is someone who is dedicated to their profession and is passionate about teaching. They possess certain characteristics that enable them to connect with their students and help them learn in an engaging and effective manner. In this article, we will discuss some of the key characteristics of a good teacher.

1. Good communication skills: A good teacher is an effective communicator. They are able to convey their ideas and instructions clearly and in a way that is easy to understand. They are also good listeners, and they take the time to listen to their students' questions and concerns.

2. Patience: A good teacher is patient with their students. They understand that learning can be a process that takes time, and they are willing to work with their students at their own pace. They do not get frustrated easily and are always willing to provide additional support and guidance when needed.

3. Adaptability: A good teacher is adaptable. They are able to adjust their teaching style to suit the needs of their students. They are also willing to try new teaching methods and technologies to keep their students engaged and interested.

4. Passion for teaching: A good teacher is passionate about teaching. They have a love for their subject matter and are excited to share their knowledge with their students. They are also committed to helping their students succeed and are willing to go above and beyond to ensure their success.

5. Empathy: A good teacher is empathetic. They are able to understand their students' feelings and concerns and are able to provide a supportive and nurturing environment. They are also able to relate to their students on a personal level, which helps to build strong relationships.

6. Creativity: A good teacher is creative. They are able to come up with innovative ways to teach their subject matter and keep their students engaged. They are also open to new ideas and are willing to try new things in the classroom.

7. High expectations: A good teacher has high expectations for their students. They believe that their students are capable of achieving great things, and they provide the support and guidance needed to help them reach their full potential.

8. Organization skills: A good teacher is organized. They are able to manage their time effectively and have a well-structured lesson plan. They also keep track of their students' progress and provide regular feedback to help them improve.

9. Sense of humor: A good teacher has a sense of humor. They are able to make their students laugh and create a positive and enjoyable learning environment. They also use humor to help their students remember important information.

In conclusion, a good teacher possesses certain characteristics that enable them to connect with their students and help them learn in an engaging and effective manner. They are dedicated to their profession and are passionate about teaching. They have good communication skills, are patient, adaptable, and creative, and have high expectations for their students. They are empathetic, organized, and have a sense of humor. These characteristics make for a great teacher, and they are essential to ensuring that students receive a high-quality education.

What makes a good learner?

Learning is an essential part of life. We learn new things every day, from the simplest tasks to the most complex ideas. However, not everyone is a good learner. Some people struggle to understand new concepts, while others seem to absorb knowledge effortlessly. So, what makes a good learner? In this article, we will discuss the characteristics of a good learner.

1. Curiosity

Good learners are naturally curious. They have a strong desire to learn and explore new ideas. They ask questions and seek answers to satisfy their curiosity. Curiosity is a vital characteristic of a good learner because it motivates them to seek knowledge and understand the world around them.

2. Openness

Good learners are open-minded. They are willing to consider new ideas and perspectives, even if they contradict their existing beliefs. They are not afraid to challenge their own assumptions and are open to changing their minds when presented with new evidence. Openness is important because it allows learners to broaden their horizons and gain a deeper understanding of the world.

3. Persistence

Good learners are persistent. They do not give up easily when faced with challenges. They are willing to put in the time and effort required to master a new skill or concept. They understand that learning takes time and practice, and they are willing to persevere through the difficult times. Persistence is crucial because it helps learners overcome obstacles and achieve their goals.

4. Adaptability

Good learners are adaptable. They are able to adjust their learning style to suit different situations or challenges. They understand that not all learning experiences are the same and that they may need to approach each one differently. Adaptability is essential because it allows learners to be flexible and responsive to changing circumstances.

5. Critical thinking

Good learners are critical thinkers. They are able to analyze and evaluate information to make informed decisions. They do not accept information blindly, but instead, they question it and seek evidence to support it. Critical thinking is important because it enables learners to make sense of the world and make informed decisions.

6. Active listening

Good learners are active listeners. They pay attention to details and are able to ask thoughtful questions. They do not just hear what is being said, but they actively engage with the information presented. Active listening is crucial because it helps learners to understand and retain information.

7. Self-awareness

Good learners are self-aware. They understand their own learning style, strengths, and weaknesses. They are able to identify their areas of improvement and work on them. Self-awareness is important because it helps learners to optimize their learning experience and achieve their goals.

8. Time management

Good learners are good at managing their time. They prioritize their learning goals and make time for them. They understand that learning is a continuous process and that they need to invest time and effort into it. Time management is essential because it helps learners to stay organized and focused on their learning goals.

9. Collaboration

Good learners are collaborative. They are able to work well with others to achieve common learning goals. They share their knowledge and skills with others and are willing to learn from them. Collaboration is important because it enables learners to learn from others and gain a deeper understanding of the topic.

10. Reflection

Good learners regularly reflect on their learning experiences. They use their experiences to improve their future learning. They identify what worked well and what didn't and make changes accordingly. Reflection is important because it helps learners to optimize their learning experience and achieve their goals.

In conclusion, good learners possess several characteristics that enable them to learn effectively. Curiosity, openness, persistence, adaptability, critical thinking, active listening, self-awareness, time management, collaboration, and reflection are all essential characteristics of a good learner. By cultivating these characteristics, anyone can become a successful learner and achieve their learning goals.

What Should I Know About My ESL Students?

Teaching English as a Second Language (ESL) can be a rewarding and challenging experience. As an ESL teacher, it is important to understand the needs of your students and be aware of the various factors that can affect their learning. This essay will discuss six key points that an ESL teacher should consider when teaching their students: cultural background, language proficiency, learning styles, motivation, age, and educational goals. By understanding these points, an ESL teacher can create a successful learning environment for their students.

Cultural Background

The cultural background of ESL students can have a significant impact on their learning. It is important for teachers to understand the culture of their students in order to create a comfortable learning environment. For example, some cultures may place a greater emphasis on respect for authority figures, while others may be more open to discussion and debate. Additionally, understanding the cultural values of students can help teachers to better understand their motivations and expectations. By taking the time to learn about the culture of their students, teachers can create a more effective learning environment.

Language Proficiency

The language proficiency of ESL students is another important factor to consider. Students may have varying levels of proficiency in English, ranging from beginner to advanced. It is important for teachers to assess the language proficiency of their students in order to create an appropriate lesson plan. For example, a beginner student may need more basic instruction and practice with pronunciation and grammar, while an advanced student may benefit from more complex topics and activities. By understanding the language proficiency of their students, teachers can create lessons that are tailored to their needs.

Learning Styles

The learning styles of ESL students should also be taken into account. Different students may have different preferences for how they learn best. Some may prefer visual aids such as pictures or diagrams, while others may prefer auditory or kinesthetic activities. By understanding the learning styles of their students, teachers can create lessons that are engaging and effective.

Motivation

Motivation is another important factor for ESL teachers to consider. Students may have different reasons for wanting to learn English, such as wanting to communicate with family members or pursue higher education. It is important for teachers to understand the motivations of their students in order to create lessons that are meaningful and relevant. By connecting the lessons to the motivations of their students, teachers can create a more engaging learning environment.

Age

The age of ESL students is also an important factor to consider. Younger students may need more structure and guidance than older students, while older students may benefit from more independent activities. Additionally, younger students may need more repetition and practice in order to master a concept, while older students may be able to move on more quickly. By understanding the age of their students, teachers can create lessons that are appropriate for their level of development.

Educational Goals

Finally, it is important for teachers to understand the educational goals of their students. Some students may be looking to improve their conversational skills, while others may be preparing for an exam or university entrance test. By understanding the educational goals of their students, teachers can create lessons that are tailored to their needs and help them reach their goals.

In conclusion, teaching ESL can be a rewarding and challenging experience. As an ESL teacher, it is important to understand the needs of your students and be aware of the various factors that can affect their learning. By considering cultural background, language proficiency, learning styles, motivation, age, and educational goals, teachers can create a successful learning environment for their students. With this knowledge, ESL teachers can help their students reach their goals and become proficient in English.

Why do adults learn English?

Learning English as an adult can be a daunting task, but it is a worthwhile endeavor that can open up a world of opportunities. There are many reasons why adults choose to learn English, such as to improve their job prospects, to be able to communicate with people from different cultures, and to gain access to educational resources. In this essay, I will discuss six reasons why adults learn English and the benefits they can gain from doing so.

To Improve Job Prospects

Adults often learn English in order to improve their job prospects. English is the language of international business, and many employers require their employees to have a certain level of proficiency in the language. For those who are looking for a job in a foreign country, learning English can be essential for success. Additionally, many employers prefer to hire those who have a good command of the language, as it shows that they are willing to invest in their own development and are open to new challenges.

To Communicate with People from Different Cultures

Another reason why adults learn English is to be able to communicate with people from different cultures. English is the most widely spoken language in the world, and it is used as a lingua franca in many countries. By learning English, adults can make connections with people from different backgrounds and cultures, which can lead to new opportunities and experiences. Additionally, learning English can help adults understand different perspectives and gain insight into other cultures.

To Gain Access to Educational Resources

Adults also learn English in order to gain access to educational resources. Many universities and colleges offer courses in English, and having a good command of the language can make it easier for adults to pursue higher education. Additionally, many books, articles, and other educational materials are written in English, so learning the language can open up a world of knowledge and understanding.

To Travel Abroad

Adults also learn English in order to travel abroad. English is the official language of many countries, and being able to communicate in the language can make it much easier for adults to navigate their way around a foreign country. Additionally, learning English can help adults make connections with locals and gain insight into the culture of the country they are visiting.

To Enjoy Entertainment in English

Adults also learn English in order to enjoy entertainment in the language. Movies, television shows, music, and books are all available in English, and being able to understand them can open up a world of entertainment options. Additionally, learning English can help adults appreciate the nuances of the language and understand jokes and references that they may not have been able to understand before.

To Feel More Connected to the World

Finally, adults learn English in order to feel more connected to the world. By learning the language, adults can understand news from around the world and engage in conversations with people from different cultures. Additionally, learning English can help adults feel more confident when interacting with people from other countries and make them feel more connected to the global community.

In conclusion, there are many reasons why adults learn English, such as to improve their job prospects, to be able to communicate with people from different cultures, and to gain access to educational resources. Learning English can also help adults travel abroad more easily, enjoy entertainment in the language, and feel more connected to the world. For these reasons, learning English as an adult can be a rewarding experience that can open up a world of opportunities.

2-5

Differences every teacher should know about Adults and Children

When it comes to teaching, it is important to understand the differences between adults and children. While there are many similarities between the two, there are also many differences that every teacher should be aware of. This essay will discuss six key differences between adults and children that every teacher should know in order to effectively teach their students.

Different Learning Styles

Children tend to learn best through hands-on activities and visual aids, while adults are more likely to learn through lectures and discussions. Children are often more easily distracted than adults, so it is important for teachers to keep their lessons interesting and engaging. Additionally, children have shorter attention spans than adults, so teachers should break up their lessons into smaller chunks and provide frequent breaks.

Different Motivations

Children are often motivated by rewards and praise, while adults are more likely to be motivated by intrinsic factors such as a sense of accomplishment or a desire to learn something new. Teachers should be aware of this difference when designing their lessons and should strive to provide meaningful rewards for their students. Additionally, teachers should be aware that adults may be more resistant to change than children, so they should be patient and understanding when introducing new concepts.

Different Levels of Maturity

Children are still developing their cognitive and emotional skills, so they may not always understand the implications of their actions or be able to control their emotions as well as adults. Teachers should be aware of this difference and should strive to provide a safe and supportive environment for their students. Additionally, teachers should be patient with their students and provide them with the guidance and support they need to develop their skills.

Different Levels of Experience

Adults often have more life experience than children, which can give them a better understanding of certain concepts or ideas. Teachers should take advantage of this by encouraging their adult students to share their experiences and insights with the class. Additionally, teachers should be aware that adults may have different expectations for their learning experience than children, so they should strive to meet those expectations in order to ensure a successful learning experience for all students.

Different Levels of Responsibility

Adults are often more responsible than children, as they have more experience managing their own lives and making decisions. Teachers should take advantage of this by assigning more responsibility to their adult students and allowing them to take ownership of their learning experience. Additionally, teachers should be aware that adults may have other commitments outside of school, such as work or family obligations, so they should strive to be flexible and accommodating when possible.

Different Levels of Engagement

Children are often more eager to participate in activities than adults, so teachers should strive to create engaging lessons that will keep their students interested and motivated. Additionally, teachers should be aware that adults may need more time to process information or ask questions than children, so they should allow for plenty of time for discussion and reflection during their lessons.

In conclusion, it is important for teachers to understand the differences between adults and children in order to effectively teach their students. Adults and children have different learning styles, motivations, levels of maturity, experience, responsibility, and engagement with the material, so teachers should strive to accommodate these differences in order to ensure a successful learning experience for all students. By understanding the differences between adults and children, teachers can create an environment where everyone can learn and grow together.

English language levels

The English language is a complex and ever-evolving language, and there are many different levels of proficiency. From basic conversational English to advanced academic English, there are a variety of levels that can be achieved. In this essay, I will discuss the six main levels of English language proficiency, including beginner, elementary, pre-intermediate, intermediate, upper-intermediate, and advanced.

Beginner

The beginner level of English language proficiency is for those who are just starting to learn the language. At this level, students are able to understand and use basic phrases and sentences. They are able to introduce themselves and ask simple questions. They can also understand basic instructions and directions. At this level, students are able to understand simple conversations in English, but they may not be able to participate in them.

Elementary

The elementary level of English language proficiency is for those who have a basic understanding of the language. At this level, students are able to understand and use more complex sentences and phrases. They are able to ask and answer questions about familiar topics. They can also understand more complex instructions and directions. At this level, students are able to understand and participate in conversations about everyday topics.

Pre-Intermediate

The pre-intermediate level of English language proficiency is for those who have a good understanding of the language. At this level, students are able to understand and use more complex grammar structures. They are able to ask and answer questions about a variety of topics. They can also understand more complex instructions and directions. At this level, students are able to understand and participate in conversations about a variety of topics.

Intermediate

The intermediate level of English language proficiency is for those who have a good understanding of the language. At this level, students are able to understand and use more complex grammar structures. They are able to ask and answer questions about a variety of topics with ease. They can also understand more complex instructions and directions. At this level, students are able to understand and participate in conversations about a variety of topics with ease.

Upper-Intermediate

The upper-intermediate level of English language proficiency is for those who have a very good understanding of the language. At this level, students are able to understand and use more complex grammar structures with ease. They are able to ask and answer questions about a variety of topics with ease. They can also understand more complex instructions and directions with ease. At this level, students are able to understand and participate in conversations about a variety of topics with ease.

Advanced

The advanced level of English language proficiency is for those who have an excellent understanding of the language. At this level, students are able to understand and use more complex grammar structures with ease. They are able to ask and answer questions about a variety of topics with ease. They can also understand more complex instructions and directions with ease. At this level, students are able to understand and participate in conversations about a variety of topics with ease.

In conclusion, there are six main levels of English language proficiency: beginner, elementary, pre-intermediate, intermediate, upper-intermediate, and advanced. Each level has its own set of skills that must be mastered in order to reach the next level. With practice and dedication, anyone can become proficient in the English language.

Chapter 3

English Language Teaching Methodology

English Language Methodology: A Comprehensive Exploration

Understanding and mastering the English language requires not just knowledge of grammar and vocabulary, but also a strategic approach towards learning. Over the years, numerous methods have been developed to teach English as a first language as well as a second or foreign language. This comprehensive article aims to explore the most common English language methodologies, providing insights into their history, key aspects, applications, and overall efficacy.

1. Grammar-Translation Method

Rooted in the teaching of classical languages like Latin and Greek, the Grammar-Translation Method has since been adapted for the study of modern languages, including English. Central to this approach is the study of grammar rules and the translation of sentences, often between the first language (L1) and English. While this method emphasizes the acquisition of grammatical knowledge, it is often criticized for not prioritizing speaking and listening skills.

2. Audio-Lingual Method

Emerging during World War II, the Audio-Lingual Method aimed to help military personnel acquire foreign language skills quickly and efficiently. This approach involves repetitive drills focused on learning and practicing specific patterns of English language in real-life situations, with emphasis on speaking and listening. Despite its rapid decline in popularity due to its overemphasis on memorization, the Audio-Lingual Method still has a place in specific contexts, such as short-term language immersion programs.

3. Direct Method

The Direct Method, sometimes referred to as the Natural Method, is a response to the shortcomings of the Grammar-Translation Method. Pioneered by Charles Berlitz in the late 19th century, this method champions the belief that learners of English should be exposed to the target language directly, with communication being the primary goal. Consequently, learners focus on everyday conversations, with grammar, vocabulary, and pronunciation taught in context. Although the Direct Method has its drawbacks, including the need for highly skilled teachers, it remains a popular choice in immersion-based settings.

4. Communicative Language Teaching (CLT)

CLT emerged in the 1970s as a way to better reflect real-life communication scenarios, greatly influenced by the linguistic theories of Noam Chomsky and Dell Hymes. This approach emphasizes the importance of learning English in context by focusing on practical language use, interactive activities, and task-based learning. CLT prioritizes negotiation, interaction, and cooperative learning, encouraging students to develop proficiency through problem-solving and purposeful communication.

5. Task-Based Language Teaching (TBLT)

TBLT is an offshoot of CLT that focuses on the use of language as a tool for achieving specific objectives. In TBLT, learners work together to complete tasks, such as giving directions or making travel plans, using authentic materials and real-life communication situations. This approach encourages learners to use English in ways that are purposeful and engaging, fostering fluency and flexibility in the language.

6. Content and Language Integrated Learning (CLIL)

CLIL is a dual-focused approach that integrates English language learning with the study of a particular subject, such as history, science, or literature. The goal of CLIL is to cultivate language skills as well as subject matter knowledge simultaneously, immersing students in relevant content while developing their English language capabilities. Through this technique, students gain an intrinsic motivation to learn English and are better equipped for academic and professional contexts.

English language methodologies have continued to evolve over time, often as a response to perceived shortcomings in earlier approaches. Ultimately, the most effective method for any learner depends on factors such as individual learning style, goals, cultural background, and the abilities of the teacher. Selecting the right methodology, or a combination of approaches, can make a significant difference in the success of professional, academic, or personal language goals. Regardless of the chosen method, it is essential to remember that English language learning is a lifelong journey that requires constant engagement, reinforcement, and practice.

3-2

The Grammar-Translation Method: An In-Depth Exploration

The Grammar-Translation Method, which can be traced back to the 16th century, has played a significant role in the domain of foreign language instruction. Despite contemporary teaching approaches often taking center stage, understanding the principles and application of this classic method can provide useful insights into language learning strategies. This article presents an in-depth exploration of the Grammar-Translation Method, examining its definition, origins, principles, methodological approaches, advantages, disadvantages, and relevance in modern language education.

1. Definition

The Grammar-Translation Method refers to a traditional language learning approach that emphasizes the explicit teaching of grammatical rules, syntax, and vocabulary, supplemented by translation exercises, and typically focused on reading and writing skills, rather than listening and speaking. This method encourages the rote learning of vocabulary and the explicit memorization of grammar rules, placing accuracy above communicative fluency.

2. Origins

The roots of the Grammar-Translation Method can be found in the classical teaching practices of Latin and Greek, languages that were central to European education during the 16th to 19th centuries. Initially devised to prepare scholars for the in-depth study of literary texts, this approach was later adapted to teach modern, spoken languages. Essentially, the Grammar-Translation Method served as a bridge between the traditions of classical language instruction and present-day foreign language education.

3. Principles

The Grammar-Translation Method is grounded in a few key principles:

a. Language as a system of rules: This method regards the target language as a set of grammatical rules, sentence structures, and vocabulary to be learned and memorized systematically.

b. Focus on reading and writing: Students primarily develop their reading and writing skills, often neglecting the importance of listening and speaking.

c. Explicit grammar instruction: Grammar is taught using explicit explanations, comparing and contrasting target language rules with those of the native language.

d. Translation exercises: Students practice translation as a way to apply and reinforce their understanding of grammar rules and vocabulary.

e. Deductive learning: Lessons often commence with the presentation of a grammar rule, accompanied by examples, which the learners are expected to internalize and apply to subsequent exercises.

4. Methodology

In the Grammar-Translation Method, teachers typically follow a set of routines that include:

a. Grammar explanations and comparisons: Grammar rules are presented, frequently involving comparisons of similar structures in the native language to facilitate understanding.

b. Vocabulary lists and rote learning: Students memorize extensive vocabulary lists, focusing on the target language's written forms and meanings rather than pronunciation and usage in context.

c. Translation exercises: Students translate sentences or passages from their native language to the target language and vice versa.

d. Written assignments: Homework and class tasks might involve completing fill-in-the-blank, sentence transformation, or error correction activities.

5. Advantages

Several advantages of the Grammar-Translation Method include:

a. Building a solid foundation: This approach provides students with a comprehensive understanding of the target language's grammar and vocabulary, potentially aiding in the accurate production of language.

b. Fostering analytical skills: Students often develop strong analytical skills as they work on understanding and applying grammar rules.

c. Enhancing reading proficiency: As the method emphasizes reading comprehension, students may develop a high proficiency in interpreting and comprehending written texts.

6. Disadvantages

There are some notable drawbacks to the Grammar-Translation Method:

a. Limited communicative competence: Students may struggle with oral communication, fluency, and listening comprehension due to the method's primary focus on reading and writing.

b. Lack of engagement: The method's rote learning and repetitive translation exercises can hinder motivation and interest in language learning for some students.

c. Overemphasis on accuracy: The method's strong emphasis on linguistic precision may lead students to be hesitant to communicate spontaneously, fearing errors and imperfections.

7. Relevance in Modern Language Education

While the Grammar-Translation Method has taken a backseat to more communicative and immersive strategies, it still holds value as an approach to building a strong grammatical foundation. Elements of this method can be integrated into contemporary language learning programs, providing students with a comprehensive understanding of grammatical structures while addressing their communicative needs.

The Grammar-Translation Method represents a critical link in the history of foreign language teaching, laying a foundation for understanding and using language as a system of rules and structures. Although modern approaches have shifted focus from form to function and from translation to communication, the method's importance in language education history and its potential to supplement contemporary teaching practices should not be overlooked.

The Audio-Lingual Method: A Comprehensive Overview

The audio-lingual method (ALM) is a widely employed language teaching approach that emerged in the 1940s and 1950s. Its primary objective is to help students develop speaking and listening skills through repetitive pattern practice and mimicry. The ALM fundamentally focuses on imitation, reinforcement, and habit formation, in order to facilitate the acquisition of a new language. This article will explore its history, principles, techniques, advantages, and drawbacks.

1. History of the Audio-Lingual Method

The audio-lingual method's roots can be traced back to the Second World War, when the US government needed an effective approach to train its military personnel in foreign languages rapidly. Based on behavioral psychology and linguistics, the method evolved as a direct response to the grammar-translation method, which prioritized reading and writing skills and led to limited development of conversational skills.

Pioneered by Charles Fries in the Michigan Model, the ALM gained worldwide recognition in language education. It laid the foundation for many teaching techniques we know today. By the late 1960s, the method's popularity started to wane as educational theorists began to criticize its rigidity.

2. Principles of the Audio-Lingual Method

ALM is based on critical principles drawn from psychological and linguistic theories. Some key principles include:

- Structuralism: ALM adheres to the belief that language learning should be based on understanding the structure of a language, including phonetics and grammar.

- Behaviorism: As a behaviorist approach, ALM encourages habit formation through imitation, repetition, and reinforcement.

- Skill Acquisition: Rather than memorizing explicit grammar rules, ALM promotes the development of listening and speaking skills through direct exposure and practice.

3. Key Techniques of the Audio-Lingual Method

ALM incorporates a range of techniques to enhance skills in listening, speaking, reading, and writing. Some of these techniques are:

- Dialogues and drills: Teachers utilize scripted dialogues and pattern practice drills to reinforce language structures and model pronunciation.

- Mimicry and memorization: Students are expected to mimic and memorize native speakers' pronunciation and intonation, without giving explicit attention to grammatical rules.

- Feedback and reinforcement: Immediate feedback is provided to correct errors, and positive feedback reinforces successful language use.

- Use of the target language: Almost all instruction is given in the target language, minimizing the use of the students' first language.

4. Advantages of the Audio-Lingual Method

ALM offers several advantages in language learning:

- Rapid language acquisition: Due to its focus on speaking and listening, learners can develop conversational skills in a comparatively shorter time.

- Encouragement of active participation: The method involves different types of drills that compel students to participate.
- Formation of language habits: ALM helps students develop habits in a new language through imitation, repetition, and reinforcement.
- Cultural dimension: Scripted dialogues can be used to expose learners to the cultural context of the target language.

5. Criticisms and Drawbacks of the Audio-Lingual Method

Despite its merits, the ALM has been criticized for various reasons:
- Limited creativity: Students don't get ample opportunities to use language creatively, as they primarily practice scripted dialogues.
- Overemphasis on drills: Drills can be monotonous, which may lead to reduced motivation.
- Insufficient treatment of grammar: In not addressing grammar explicitly, the ALM might impede some learners' profound understanding of the target language.
- Neglect of reading and writing skills: The heavy focus on speaking and listening skills may cause inadequacies in proficiency in reading and writing.

The audio-lingual method has contributed significantly to the contemporary understanding of language teaching. While it has various drawbacks and has been widely criticized, the method's focus on listening and speaking skills has helped countless students develop strong conversational abilities. An integration of the ALM's principles and techniques with other language teaching approaches could enhance the overall learning experience, providing the best of linguistic, communicative, and cognitive components.

Sample lesson plan: Introduction to Present Continuous Tense with Audio-Lingual Method

Duration: 1 hour
Level: Pre-intermediate
Age Group: 12-16 years old
Language Focus: Present Continuous Tense

Skills: Listening, Speaking, Reading

Objective: By the end of this lesson, students will be able to use and understand the present continuous tense in English.

Materials:
- Audio clips
- Pictures representing various actions
- Whiteboard/Chalkboard
- Markers/Chalk
- Handouts with sample sentences

Lesson Plan:

1. Warm-up (5 minutes)

- Have students introduce themselves in pairs using the following structure:

"My name is... I am... years old, and I am from...", then ask each student to present their partner to the class.

2. Introduction (5 minutes)

- Introduce the present continuous tense by briefly explaining its function in English (e.g., used to describe actions happening right now).

3. Presentation (15 minutes)

- Write examples of present continuous sentences on the board and underline the verb structure:

"She is riding a bicycle."
"They are playing soccer."
"I am reading a book."

- Draw students' attention to the present continuous structure (be+verb+ing) and explain that the verb "to be" works as an auxiliary verb.

4. Audio-lingual practice (20 minutes)

Part A - Model Conversations (10 minutes)

- Play several audio clips with conversations that demonstrate the present continuous tense.

- Have students work in pairs and practice the conversations together.

Part B - Drill exercises (10 minutes)

- Select appropriate drill exercises for the present continuous tense (e.g., repetition drills, substitution drills, and transformation drills).

- Use pictures representing various actions to help students visualize the context.

- Guide and correct students during the drill exercises, ensuring they use the present continuous tense properly.

5. Controlled practice (10 minutes)

- Distribute handouts with sample sentences.

- Teams of two students will be assigned to complete the sample sentences using the present continuous tense.

- Review and discuss the correct answers with the class once complete.

6. Wrap-up (5 minutes)

- Ask a few students to share their opinion on the lesson and what they learned about the present continuous tense.

- Offer encouragement and highlight essential points from the lesson.

Homework:

- Encourage students to practice the present continuous tense in real-life situations outside the classroom (e.g., writing an email, Facebook update, or forming spoken sentences about their current actions).

Evaluation:

- Students' performance during drill exercises and controlled practice activity will help assess their understanding and application of the present continuous tense.

A Comprehensive Guide to the Presentation, Practice, and Production (PPP) Method for Language Teaching

The Presentation, Practice, and Production (PPP) Model is an established and effective method for teaching new language skills. Utilized by language teachers across the globe, the PPP method focuses on providing effective scaffolding for learners to both introduce and reinforce language concepts within a structured framework. This comprehensive article will explore the PPP method, its key components, benefits, and potential drawbacks, while also offering insights into its implementation in the contemporary language classroom.

Section 1: A Closer Look at Presentation, Practice, and Production

1.1 Definition of the PPP Method
The PPP method is a systematic, step-by-step approach to language instruction, incorporating the presentation of new material, guided practice, and the eventual production of language skills. The ultimate

goal of the PPP method is to develop the learner's practical ability to use target language structures in authentic situations.

1.2 The Three Components
The PPP method consists of three integrated stages:

A. Presentation
- The teacher introduces new language concepts, providing explanations, examples, and contextual information
- The focus is on accuracy, as learners absorb and become familiar with the target language's rules and structures

B. Practice
- The learners engage in guided activities that aim to help them understand and apply the new language concepts
- Through repetition, feedback, and reinforcement, learners start to use the target language with increased confidence

C. Production
- Learners apply the new language skills in realistic, communicative situations
- They practice accuracy and fluency by creating genuine context for the target language's structures

Section 2: Benefits of the PPP Method

2.1 Scaffolding and Structure
The stepwise nature of the PPP method provides a clear, structured approach for learners, making it easier to assimilate and grasp new language concepts.

2.2 Focus on Accuracy and Fluency

The PPP method emphasizes the importance of both linguistic accuracy and communicative fluency, creating a balance that supports real-world language use.

2.3 Confidence Building

By progressing from a supported, structured environment to a self-directed production stage, learners gradually gain the confidence required to use the target language in authentic situations.

Section 3: Potential Drawbacks of the PPP Method

3.1 Limited Flexibility

The PPP method's structure might not be suitable for all learners, as it requires a linear progression and potentially restricts creativity.

3.2 Overemphasis on Accuracy

Some critics argue that the method's focus on accuracy may hinder the development of fluency and discourage learners from experimenting with the language.

Section 4: Best Practices and Implementation Strategies

4.1 Adapting to Different Learner Types

To ensure the effectiveness of the PPP method, consider the unique needs and preferences of your learners. Make adaptations accordingly, while maintaining the core process.

4.2 Incorporating Technology

Embrace the potential of technology, including multimedia presentations, interactive quizzes, and engaging digital resources, to enhance your lessons.

4.3 Encouraging Collaboration and Problem-Solving

Foster collaboration and problem-solving skills by incorporating pair or group work into your practice and production phases.

The PPP method has stood the test of time as an effective, favored approach to language instruction. Its sequential structure supports learners in elevating their comprehension and language usage in a systematic, confidence-building manner. By being mindful of its limitations and proactively adapting the method to the needs of individual learners, contemporary language teachers are poised to find continued success in employing the PPP model in their classrooms.

Sample Lesson Plan - Present Tense Verbs: Regular and Irregular

Objective: By the end of the lesson, students should be able to identify and use the present tense of regular and irregular verbs correctly in spoken and written English.

Materials: Whiteboard and markers, handout sheets, worksheets, projector, computer, and an audio system.

Duration: 60 minutes

Lesson overview:
1. Warm-up activity (5 minutes)
2. Presentation (15 minutes)
3. Practice (20 minutes)
4. Production (20 minutes)
5. Wrap-up/assessment (5 minutes)

1. Warm-up activity (5 minutes)

- Begin the lesson by asking students simple questions requiring answers in the present tense, e.g., "What do you do on weekends?"
- Have students pair up and discuss their daily routine, focusing on their activities during weekdays.

2. Presentation (15 minutes)

- Use the projector to present a slideshow on regular and irregular verbs in the present tense.
- Explain the rules for forming the present tense of regular verbs (e.g., adding -s, -es, or -ies) and provide examples.
- Discuss common irregular verbs (e.g., be, do, have, go) and their present tense forms.
- Introduce the concept of subject-verb agreement and highlight its importance in using present tense verbs correctly.
- Play an audio clip with examples of sentences using present tense regular and irregular verbs.

3. Practice (20 minutes)
- Hand out worksheets with fill-in-the-blank sentences and have students complete them individually.
- Walk around the classroom to monitor students' understanding and provide assistance if needed.
- Have students pair up and take turns reading their sentences aloud, focusing on the correct verb form and pronunciation.
- Ask a few volunteers to share their sentences with the class, and provide feedback on their accuracy and pronunciation.

4. Production (20 minutes)
- Split the class into small groups (3-4 students per group).
- Assign each group a role-play scenario (e.g., at a restaurant, in a classroom, or at a party) that requires them to use regular and irregular verbs in the present tense.
- Provide 10 minutes for groups to create and rehearse a 2-3 minute long dialog.
- Have each group perform their role-play in front of the class.
- While groups perform, take notes on their use of present tense verbs for feedback.

5. Wrap-up/assessment (5 minutes)

- Review key concepts from the lesson (rules for regular verbs, common irregular verbs, and subject-verb agreement).

- Address any common errors or misconceptions observed during the practice and production activities.

- Provide feedback to the groups on their role-play performances and celebrate their successes.

- Exit ticket: Students will write a sentence using a regular verb and a sentence using an irregular verb in the present tense. Collect these as they leave the class to assess overall comprehension.

The Task-based Method: Exploring Key Concepts, Components, and Applications

The Task-based Method, often referred to as Task-based Language Teaching (TBLT) or Task-based Learning (TBL), is an innovative approach to language learning which has gained considerable attention in recent years. Rooted in communicative language teaching (CLT) principles, TBLT places an emphasis on both the acquisition and practical use of language through the completion of real-life tasks that encourage learners to communicate effectively. By engaging with authentic material and focusing on the exchange of meaningful information, students gain a deeper understanding of language and foster a greater level of fluency.

This comprehensive article delves into the key concepts, components, and applications of the Task-based Method, exploring its advantages, challenges, and significance in language teaching.

I. Key Concepts and Origins

1. Background

The Task-based Method emerged in response to the growing need for functional language learning and the dissatisfaction with traditional grammar-based methodologies. Influenced by communicative language teaching, TBLT prioritizes communication, problem-solving, and real-life language use in the learning process.

2. Definition

TBLT is an approach to language teaching based on the belief that learners acquire a language best when they engage in meaningful, purposeful tasks that require the exchange of information.

3. Principles

Task-based learning is based on four main principles:

i. Communication-centered: Language learning should facilitate communication and understanding, even with imperfect grammar or vocabulary.

ii. Learner-centered: Students' interests, needs, and motivations should drive the learning process.

iii. Authenticity: Language use should reflect real-life situations and experiences.

iv. Feedback-driven: Implicit and explicit feedback is vital in helping learners improve communication and language skills.

II. Components of the Task-based Method

1. Task: A key aspect of TBLT is the design of a well-defined, engaging, and purposeful task that requires learners to use language in a practical and communicative context. Tasks can range from simple activities, such as ordering food at a restaurant, to complex problem-solving scenarios, like organizing a class project.

2. **Task Cycle: A typical TBLT lesson follows three stages: pre-task, task cycle, and language focus.**

i. Pre-task: In this stage, the teacher introduces the topic and objectives of the task, activating schema, and providing necessary language support or vocabulary.

ii. Task Cycle: The core stage, the task cycle, consists of three main parts: task, planning, and report. Students work collaboratively or individually to complete the task, using language tools and strategies. They plan and produce a report or presentation on their results or findings.

iii. Language Focus: The post-task stage, language focus, involves reflection on language use and strategies, feedback, and error correction. This stage helps students cement their learning and identify areas for improvement.

III. Applications of the Task-based Method

TBLT can be effectively implemented in various language-learning settings, such as:

1. Teaching different language skills: Task-based activities can be designed for teaching listening, speaking, reading, and writing skills.

2. Exam preparation: TBLT can be employed for test preparation, as it promotes language use in context, which is often the focus of language proficiency exams.

3. Integration with technology: Tasks may be adapted to integrate digital tools, such as videos, applications, or websites, expanding students' learning opportunities and resources.

4. Cross-cultural understanding: The Task-based Method can heighten students' awareness of cultural nuances, customs, and perspectives, enhancing their global competence.

IV. Advantages and Challenges

Advantages of TBLT include increased motivation, learner autonomy, holistic language use, and opportunities for real-life practice. Simultaneously, implementing TBLT can present challenges, such as the creation of engaging tasks, the need for teacher adaptability, consideration of mixed ability classes, and the potential struggle to find appropriate material.

In conclusion, the Task-based Method represents a paradigm shift in language learning and teaching, emphasizing authentic, meaningful communication and engaged language use. By focusing on real-world tasks, TBLT not only supports language acquisition but also fosters the development of practical skills required for global citizens. Although challenges persist, with careful planning and adaptation, TBLT has the potential to revolutionize language learning for students and educators alike.

Sample Lesson Plan:
Course: General English
Level: Intermediate
Duration: 90 minutes
Method: Task-Based Language Teaching (TBLT)
Objective: By the end of the lesson, students will be able to collaboratively plan a weekend trip using various means of transportation.
Materials: Board, markers, internet-connected devices (computer, tablet, or smartphone), projector, transportation websites

Lesson Stages:

1. Warm-up (10 minutes)
- Begin with a conversation about weekend trips. Ask students about places they have visited, their favorite trips, etc.
- Write interesting and useful vocabulary words from their responses on the board.

2. Pre-task (15 minutes)
- Divide students into groups of 3 or 4.
- Ask each group to choose a destination for a weekend trip within a reasonable distance from their city.

- Students should research transport options (e.g., car, train, bus, or plane) available to reach their chosen destination.
- Have each group list transportation options, travel times, and costs on a shared document or paper.

3. Task Cycle (40 minutes)
- Ask each group to discuss and select the best transportation option based on factors like travel time, cost, comfort, etc.
- Students should create an itinerary including transportation details, hotel booking, and local attractions.
- Encourage them to use the target vocabulary and structures studied earlier in the course.
- Monitor the groups, offer assistance, and take notes on the language used.

4. Language Focus (10 minutes)
- Discuss students' language usage during the task cycle and write examples of good usage and common errors on the board.
- Clarify any misunderstandings and provide feedback on pronunciation, grammatical structures, and vocabulary.

5. Report and Reflection (10 minutes)
- Have a representative from each group present their itinerary to the class.
- Ask the class to provide feedback on each presentation and discuss their preferred itinerary.

6. Follow-up (5 minutes)
- End the session by encouraging students to plan a real trip using the language and skills they have practiced during the lesson.

Communicative Language Teaching: A Comprehensive Overview

Language is fundamentally used for communication. Teaching methods that mimic the natural acquisition of language have gained prominence over time, and the Communicative Language Teaching (CLT) method is a prime example. Initially developed in the 1970s, CLT has become an indispensable approach within the realm of language teaching. This article aims to provide an in-depth understanding of the CLT method, its theoretical basis, its key principles, strategies, advantages, and challenges.

I. Theoretical Basis of Communicative Language Teaching

Communicative Language Teaching is informed by a number of theoretical frameworks:

1. Sociolinguistics: The study of language in its social context, sociolinguistics emphasizes that successful communication is not just about grammatical correctness but also depends on the various social situations and interactions.

2. Functional-Notional Approach: This approach identifies communicative purposes as the center of language learning, focusing on the reason why people use language and the meaning they intend to convey.

3. Interactional Competence: Another key tenet of CLT; it emphasizes not only linguistic competence but also an understanding of sociocultural contexts and the ability to use language effectively in various social scenarios.

II. Principles of Communicative Language Teaching

1. Authentic Communication: CLT prioritizes the use of genuine, meaningful language and real-life contexts in its teaching materials and practices.

2. Fluency Over Accuracy: While accuracy is important, CLT largely focuses on developing fluency, emphasizing the need to develop language skills that are usable and functional in everyday communication.

3. Student Centeredness: CLT is student-centered, promoting active and participatory learning and fostering collaboration, negotiation, and problem-solving among learners.

4. Integrated Skills: CLT aims to develop all four language skills – listening, speaking, reading, and writing – in an integrated and balanced manner.

5. Task-Based Learning: In CLT, learning typically occurs through engaging in authentic tasks, aimed at facilitating the practical use of the language while developing comprehension and production skills.

III. Strategies and Techniques in Communicative Language Teaching

Some common strategies and techniques associated with CLT include:

1. Role-plays and simulations: These activities provide opportunities for students to practice language in a safe, controlled environment that closely mirrors real-life situations.

2. Cooperative learning: Activities such as group work and pair work encourage students to practice their language skills and develop interpersonal communication abilities.

3. Information gap activities: These tasks require students to exchange information to complete a task, thereby promoting listening and speaking skills.

4. Communicative games: Language games can provide enjoyable, low-pressure practice opportunities for students.

5. Giving and receiving feedback: Immediate and constructive feedback is essential for shaping communicative competence and reinforcing correct language usage.

IV. Advantages of the Communicative Language Teaching Method

1. Focus on Real-Life Communication: This gives learners a higher chance of success in real-life interactions.

2. Motivation: Learners are often more motivated as they see the direct application of their language skills.

3. Flexibility: CLT can be adapted to different contexts, learner proficiency levels, and learning goals.

4. Integrated Skill Development: Proficiency in all four language skills is better achieved through the balanced and integrated approach of CLT.

V. Challenges of Communicative Language Teaching

1. Teacher Preparation: Many teachers require additional training to adjust to the CLT approach.

2. Lack of Resources: Adopting CLT can be resource-intensive, and in many cases, the required materials may not always be locally available or affordable.

3. Cultural Issues: Some learners may experience difficulty in adapting to the more interactive and student-centered approach of CLT due to cultural barriers.

4. Assessment: It can be challenging to design assessments that accurately measure a learner's proficiency and communicative competence.

Despite its challenges, Communicative Language Teaching remains an essential method for helping students develop their language skills. Its emphasis on real-life communication, learner participation, and integrated skill development leads to greater motivation and proficiency among students. Both new and experienced language teachers can benefit from incorporating the principles, strategies, and techniques of CLT into their practice to create more engaging, effective, and enjoyable learning experiences.

Sample lesson plan:
Title: Introducing Daily Routines
Objective: To enable students to speak about their daily routines in English using the present simple tense and time expressions.
Level: Beginner (A1)
Duration: 60 minutes
Language Skills: Speaking, Listening, Vocabulary
Teaching Aids: Handout, whiteboard, flashcards, audio file, internet access

Lesson Plan:

1. Warm-Up (5 minutes)
Activity: Engaging quick activity
- Ask learners to get into pairs.
- Distribute a set of flashcards with time expressions (e.g., in the morning, at noon, in the evening) to each pair.
- The pairs will discuss and guess which part of the day each time expression refers to.

- Bring the class together and write down the results shared by each pair on the whiteboard.

2. Presentation (15 minutes)
Activity: Introducing daily routine vocabulary
- Show the class a short video about someone's daily routine.
- After watching the video, list the activities from the video on the whiteboard.
- As a class, identify the verbs (e.g., wake up, eat breakfast, brush teeth).
- Teach the relevant vocabulary by defining each activity/verb and using visuals or gestures.

3. Controlled Practice (15 minutes)
Activity: Pair work matching game
- Distribute a handout with a list of daily routine activities in one column and pictures in the other column.
- In pairs, students match the verbs to the corresponding pictures.
- Pair up the pairs to check their answers, then provide them with the correct answers.

4. Guided Practice (10 minutes)
Activity: Time expressions practice
- Display a daily routine timeline on the whiteboard.
- Select a student and ask him/her to describe an activity from the timeline.
- The rest of the class guesses which time of day the activity takes place.
- Swap roles and continue until all students have had a chance to participate.

5. Free Practice (10 minutes)
Activity: Role play
- Have students form pairs.

- Assign each student a role: "Interviewer" or "Interviewee."
- Interviewers will ask questions to find out about the Interviewee's daily routine (e.g., What time do you wake up? When do you have lunch?).
- After 5 minutes, have students switch roles.

6. Wrap-Up (5 minutes)

Activity: Sharing

- Invite some students to share a surprising or interesting detail they found out about their partner's daily routine.
- Review the new vocabulary and time expressions as a class.

Homework: Ask students to write a paragraph describing their own daily routines using the new vocabulary and time expressions learned in class.

Embracing the Power of the Community Language Learning Method

The Community Language Learning (CLL) method, a brainchild of Charles A. Curran, has provided a revolutionary approach to language learning for almost half a century. Developed in the 1970s, it emphasizes interaction, cooperation, and learning in a community atmosphere. As a learner-centered model, it stands in stark contrast to traditional teacher-dominated classrooms. In this article, we will delve into the history, key principles, advantages, disadvantages, and practical applications of the CLL method, providing a comprehensive understanding of this influential teaching strategy.

1. History and Origin:

Charles A. Curran, an American Jesuit priest and professor of psychology, was the mastermind behind the CLL method. He brought the concept to life as a part of humanistic psychology, embracing the tenets of counseling and non-directive teaching. Curran sought to create a safe and supportive learning environment, as opposed to the anxiety-inducing atmosphere some students experience in traditional language classrooms. Inspired by Carl Rogers' Person-Centered Approach to counseling, Curran's innovation became an essential element in the Communicative Language Teaching movement that would follow.

2. Key Principles of the CLL Method:

a. The Learner as a Whole Person: CLL places a strong emphasis on addressing a student's emotional, intellectual, and social needs. The method acknowledges the importance of creating a low-anxiety learning environment where students feel comfortable expressing their thoughts and doubts.

b. The Teacher as Counselor: Teachers take on the role of a counselor, guiding the learning process and fostering a non-threatening atmosphere. The educator becomes an active listener, creating a safe space for students to explore the language.

c. Group Learning: Students work in small groups and support each other in learning. Cooperation and collaboration form the backbone of the community atmosphere, enhancing both motivation and engagement.

d. Learning through Interaction: Students learn by translating and interpreting their thoughts within the context of real-life situations, enabling them to actively engage with the language.

e. Self-Reflection and Evaluation: CLL encourages students to assess their learning progress and be aware of their needs and strengths. This self-evaluation leads to increased motivation and self-directed learning.

3. Advantages of the CLL Method:

a. Reduced Anxiety: The supportive environment helps students overcome language anxiety, giving them the confidence to participate actively.

b. Enhanced Motivation: Students are more likely to stay motivated when they work cooperatively and receive support from their peers.

c. Improved Communication Skills: Real-life interactions help students develop their speaking, listening, and interpersonal skills.

d. Increased Autonomy: The focus on self-evaluation encourages learners to take responsibility for their learning, fostering self-directed growth.

e. Cultural Sensitivity: CLL often incorporates cultural elements, promoting understanding and empathy.

4. Disadvantages of the CLL Method:

a. Limited Structure: Some students may struggle with the lack of a fixed curriculum or structure, making it difficult for them to gauge their progress.

b. Inconsistency in Language Use: Due to the focus on group interaction, students might adopt their peers' errors while practicing.

c. Teacher Training: Finding teachers who are trained in applying the CLL method can be challenging.

5. Practical Applications:

a. Circles of Interaction: Arranging classroom seating in a circle promotes equal involvement and interaction among students.

b. Translation Activities: Students can collaboratively translate authentic texts or conversations, discussing different ways to express themselves.

c. Self-Evaluation and Goal Setting: Encourage learners to develop a learning plan and reflect on their progress.

d. Reflective Listening: Teach students the importance of active listening and empathy in communication, enhancing their interpersonal skills.

The Community Language Learning method remains a powerful teaching approach, fostering a supportive and collaborative environment that embraces the whole person. While it has its drawbacks, its undeniable benefits have made it a staple in modern language education. As learners and educators continue to strive for better methods in language acquisition, the concept of community and interaction will likely remain central to new approaches to come.

Sample Lesson Plan
English Lesson for Beginner Learners – Community Language Learning Method

Objective:
* Learners will improve their speaking, listening, and understanding skills in English by engaging in activities designed to build and support a community learning environment.

Materials:
* Chart paper or whiteboard
* Markers
* Word cards
* Smartphone or computer to record and play back audio

Duration: 60 minutes

I. Warm-up activity (10 minutes)

A. Introduction and greetings (5 minutes)
1. Greet students warmly and encourage them to greet each other.
2. Ask students to share some information about themselves in groups of 2 or 3 to help create a relaxed and trusting atmosphere.

B. Group formation (5 minutes)
1. Direct students to form groups of 4-5 members.
2. Ask them to select one person to be the Scribe, whose job will be to write all conversations on the chart paper or whiteboard, and another person as the Recorder, who will be in charge of recording and playing back the audio.

II. Topic selection and brainstorming (10 minutes)

A. Introduce a list of potential topics (e.g., daily routines, hobbies, local events) (5 minutes)
B. Have students vote and choose one for the day's lesson.

C. Encourage students to brainstorm and discuss the topic within their group while the Scribe writes down the conversation.

III. Vocabulary building activity (15 minutes)

A. Instruct the recorder to play short sections of the recorded conversation (10 minutes)
1. After each section, pause the recording so learners can discuss and identify new/unknown words in the conversation.
2. Help students understand the meanings and provide correct pronunciation.
B. Word cards activity (5 minutes)
1. Write each new vocabulary word on a card and give it to the respective group.
2. Students pair up within their group and practice using these words in conversations related to the topic.

IV. Building sentences and discussion (20 minutes)

A. Direct students to create full sentences using the new vocabulary words (10 minutes)
1. Encourage them to make sentences related to their personal experiences or opinions on the topic.
2. Monitor groups and offer assistance if required.
B. Whole class discussion (10 minutes)
1. Ask each group to share some of their sentences with the entire class.
2. Encourage students to ask questions or add their thoughts, fostering a supportive and interactive learning environment.

V. Conclusion (5 minutes)

A. Recap and reflection

1. Spend a few minutes going over the main points covered in the lesson and reviewing the vocabulary.

2. Ask students to reflect on their learning and share what they enjoyed or found challenging about the lesson.

B. Ending

1. Thank students for their hard work and participation.

2. Remind them to practice the new vocabulary regularly to reinforce their learning.

3-8

Community Language Learning

Community Language Learning (CLL) is an innovative and student-centered approach to language learning that places a strong emphasis on building a supportive and collaborative community within the classroom. Developed by Charles A. Curran in the 1970s, CLL aims to create a comfortable and non-threatening environment for language learners, allowing them to develop their language skills through meaningful interactions and authentic communication.

At the heart of CLL is the belief that language learning is more than just acquiring vocabulary and grammar rules; it is about developing the ability to effectively communicate in real-life situations. In traditional language learning approaches, learners often feel pressured to perform and make mistakes in front of their peers, leading to anxiety and inhibiting their progress. CLL seeks to address this issue by creating a supportive community of learners who help and support each other throughout the language learning process.

One of the key elements of CLL is the role of the "knower" or the language counselor. The language counselor, usually a fluent speaker of the target language, acts as a facilitator and guide for the learners. They provide linguistic and emotional support, helping learners express themselves and understand the target language in a comfortable and non-judgmental environment. The language counselor also encourages learners to take risks and make mistakes, emphasizing that errors are a natural part of the language learning process.

In CLL, the learning process begins with the language counselor and the learners engaging in a dialogue in the learners' native language. This initial conversation helps establish rapport and build trust between the learners and the language counselor. The learners then express their thoughts and ideas in their native language, using gestures and non-verbal cues to convey meaning.

Once the learners feel comfortable, they can start to express themselves in the target language. The language counselor acts as an intermediary, translating and paraphrasing the learners' expressions into the target language. This process, known as "translanguaging," allows learners to bridge the gap between their native language and the target language, gradually building their proficiency in the target language.

Throughout the CLL process, learners are encouraged to reflect on their language learning experiences and discuss their progress with their peers and the language counselor. This reflective practice helps learners develop metacognitive skills, enabling them to analyze and understand their own learning strategies and make adjustments accordingly. Learners also have the opportunity to provide feedback to their peers, fostering a sense of collaboration and mutual support within the classroom.

Another important aspect of CLL is the use of authentic materials and real-life situations. Learners engage in role-plays, simulations, and other interactive activities that mimic real-world communication. This approach allows learners to practice their language skills in a meaningful and contextually relevant manner, improving their ability to use the target language in real-life situations.

CLL also acknowledges the importance of learners' affective factors, such as motivation, self-esteem, and confidence. By creating a supportive and inclusive learning community, CLL helps learners feel more comfortable and confident in expressing themselves in the target language. This, in turn, enhances their motivation and engagement, leading to more effective language learning outcomes.

It is worth noting that CLL is not without its challenges. Creating a supportive and collaborative learning community requires time and effort, both from the language counselor and the learners. Additionally, the role of the language counselor can be demanding, as they need to balance their facilitation role with providing linguistic support and guidance.

Despite these challenges, CLL has been widely recognized and implemented in various language learning contexts around the world. Its student-centered and community-oriented approach has proven to be effective in fostering language proficiency, developing communication skills, and promoting intercultural understanding.

In conclusion, Community Language Learning is an innovative and student-centered approach to language learning. By creating a supportive and collaborative community within the classroom, CLL provides learners with a comfortable and non-threatening environment to develop their language skills. Through dialogue, translanguaging, reflection, and authentic communication, learners are able to build their proficiency in the target language and develop the confidence and motivation to use it in real-life situations. CLL has proven to be a successful approach in language learning, promoting effective communication, intercultural understanding, and the development of lifelong language skills.

The Silent Way

The Silent Way is an innovative language teaching method that emphasizes learner autonomy and active participation. Developed by Caleb Gattegno in the 1960s, this approach focuses on creating a supportive learning environment where students take an active role in their language learning process. The central concept behind the Silent Way is that learners should discover and internalize the language themselves, rather than being spoon-fed by the teacher. In this article, we will explore the key principles, techniques, advantages, and challenges associated with the Silent Way teaching method.

Principles of the Silent Way:

1. Learner-Centered Approach: The Silent Way places the learner at the center of the learning process. Teachers act as facilitators rather than instructors, guiding students to discover and explore the language on their own.

2. Cognitive Engagement: The method encourages learners to actively engage their minds and think critically. Students are encouraged to hypothesize, analyze, and experiment with the language to develop their own understanding.

3. Learning in Context: The Silent Way emphasizes the use of meaningful, contextualized language. Students learn language structures and vocabulary in authentic, relevant situations, allowing for better retention and application.

4. Self-Correction and Self-Evaluation: Learners are encouraged to correct their own mistakes and evaluate their progress. This promotes learner autonomy and builds confidence in their own ability to learn and improve.

Techniques of the Silent Way:

1. Fidel Charts: Fidel charts are visual aids that represent the sounds of the target language. They help students associate sounds with specific symbols and facilitate pronunciation practice.

2. Word Charts: Word charts consist of color-coded word cards that represent vocabulary items. These charts enable students to manipulate and organize words to form sentences and understand grammar structures.

3. Cuisenaire Rods: Cuisenaire rods are colorful, manipulative blocks of varying sizes. These rods are used to represent language concepts, such as word stress, sentence stress, and sentence structure. They provide a hands-on, visual way for learners to understand and internalize language patterns.

4. Minimal Pair Drill: Minimal pair drills involve contrasting words that differ by only one sound. By focusing on these minimal differences, learners develop their ability to distinguish and produce accurate sounds.

Advantages of the Silent Way:

1. Learner Autonomy: The Silent Way empowers learners to take control of their own learning process. Students become more independent and responsible for their progress, leading to greater motivation and engagement.

2. Active Participation: The method encourages students to actively participate in the learning process. Learners are given opportunities to experiment and make their own discoveries, fostering a deeper understanding of the language.

3. Critical Thinking Skills: The Silent Way promotes critical thinking skills by encouraging learners to analyze and problem-solve language challenges independently. This helps develop their ability to think creatively and adapt to different language situations.

4. Pronunciation Development: The focus on accurate pronunciation through fidel charts and minimal pair drills helps learners develop a better understanding of the sound system of the target language.

Challenges of the Silent Way:

1. Initial Learning Curve: The Silent Way requires a shift in traditional teaching roles, which may be challenging for both teachers and learners initially. Teachers need to become skilled facilitators, while learners need to adapt to a more self-directed learning environment.

2. Teacher Competence: Teachers need to have a strong understanding of the method and its techniques to effectively implement the Silent Way. They must be able to create a supportive and engaging learning environment that fosters independent learning.

3. Time-Intensive: The Silent Way may be time-consuming due to the

emphasis on individualized learning and self-correction. Teachers need to allocate sufficient time for students to explore and experiment with the language.

The Silent Way is a learner-centered language teaching method that promotes learner autonomy, active participation, and critical thinking skills. By creating a supportive learning environment and providing students with the tools they need to discover and internalize the language, the Silent Way method offers a unique approach to language acquisition. Although it may present initial challenges, the benefits of learner empowerment and deeper language understanding make it a valuable method for language educators to consider.

Suggestopaedia

An Innovative Teaching Method for Optimal Learning

In the realm of education, there is a constant quest to find innovative teaching methods that facilitate optimal learning and retention. One such method that has gained prominence in recent years is Suggestopaedia. Developed by Bulgarian psychiatrist and educator, Dr. Georgi Lozanov, in the 1970s, Suggestopaedia is a unique teaching approach that aims to enhance learning by creating an optimal psychological and physiological state in students. This comprehensive article will explore the principles, techniques, benefits, and criticisms of Suggestopaedia, providing a detailed understanding of this teaching method.

Principles of Suggestopaedia:

Suggestopaedia is based on the following fundamental principles:

1. Suggestion: The power of suggestion is central to Suggestopaedia. It utilizes verbal and non-verbal suggestions to create a positive and relaxed learning environment, enhancing students' receptivity to new information.

2. Desuggestion: In order to overcome any preconceived notions or barriers to learning, Suggestopaedia employs desuggestion techniques. These techniques help to eradicate limiting beliefs and negative associations, thereby creating a fertile ground for learning.

3. Relaxation: A relaxed state of mind and body is crucial for effective learning. Suggestopaedia incorporates relaxation techniques, such as music, to induce a state of deep relaxation in students, enabling them to absorb information more readily.

4. Peripheral Learning: Unlike traditional teaching methods that focus solely on the conscious mind, Suggestopaedia taps into the power of the subconscious through peripheral learning. This involves exposing students to additional sensory stimuli, such as background music or visuals, to enhance the learning experience.

Techniques of Suggestopaedia:

Suggestopaedia utilizes a range of techniques to optimize the learning process. Some of the key techniques employed include:

1. Concert Sessions: These sessions involve playing background music, specifically composed to induce a relaxed state of mind, while students engage in learning activities. The music acts as a catalyst, enhancing the students' receptivity to new information.

2. Dramatized Texts: Suggestopaedia incorporates the use of dramatized texts, where the teacher reads aloud in a melodious and expressive manner. This technique helps to capture the students' attention, making the learning experience more engaging and memorable.

3. Positive Atmosphere: Creating a positive and supportive atmosphere is essential in Suggestopaedia. Teachers use encouraging language and provide constant positive reinforcement to boost students'

self-confidence and motivation.

4. Baroque Music: Suggestopaedia often employs the use of Baroque music during learning sessions. The specific rhythmic patterns and harmonies of Baroque music have been found to stimulate the brain and enhance memory retention.

Benefits of Suggestopaedia:

Suggestopaedia offers several advantages over traditional teaching methods:

1. Increased Retention: By creating a relaxed and positive learning environment, Suggestopaedia improves students' retention and recall of information. The combination of suggestion, relaxation, and peripheral learning optimizes the brain's receptivity to new knowledge.

2. Enhanced Motivation: The use of music, dramatized texts, and positive reinforcement in Suggestopaedia fosters a high level of motivation in students. This heightened motivation leads to greater engagement and active participation in the learning process.

3. Reduction of Anxiety: Suggestopaedia's emphasis on relaxation techniques helps alleviate anxiety and stress commonly associated with learning. Students feel more at ease, which enables them to focus and absorb information more effectively.

4. Creative and Holistic Learning: Suggestopaedia encourages a holistic approach to learning that encompasses various sensory modalities. By integrating music, drama, and visual stimuli, it stimulates creativity and enables students to explore different avenues of understanding.

Criticism and Limitations:

While Suggestopaedia has shown promising results, it is not without its criticisms and limitations:

1. Limited Applicability: Suggestopaedia has primarily been used in language learning contexts. Its effectiveness in other subject areas or disciplines is yet to be thoroughly explored.

2. Lack of Scientific Validation: Some critics argue that the scientific evidence supporting Suggestopaedia is limited. While there have been positive anecdotal reports, more rigorous research is needed to validate its claims.

3. Practical Implementation: Implementing Suggestopaedia requires a dedicated and skilled instructor who can effectively employ its techniques. This can pose challenges in traditional educational settings with limited resources and training opportunities.

Suggestopaedia stands as an innovative and holistic teaching method that aims to optimize the learning experience. By incorporating suggestion, relaxation, peripheral learning, and music, it creates an environment conducive to enhanced retention, motivation, and creativity. While further research and practical implementation may be necessary, Suggestopaedia offers a unique approach to teaching that has the potential to revolutionize traditional educational practices.

3-11

The Lexical Approach

Enhancing Language Learning Through Vocabulary

In the realm of language teaching and learning, various methods and approaches have been developed over the years to help learners acquire a new language effectively. One such approach that has gained prominence is the lexical approach. This comprehensive method focuses on the importance of vocabulary in language acquisition, emphasizing the significance of words and phrases in communication. In this article, we delve into the principles, key features, and benefits of the lexical approach in teaching and learning a foreign language.

Principles of the Lexical Approach:

The lexical approach is rooted in the belief that vocabulary plays a central role in language learning. It recognizes that languages are primarily composed of lexis, i.e., words and phrases, and that mastering lexical chunks is crucial for effective communication. Rather than focusing solely on grammar rules and sentence structures, the lexical approach emphasizes the need for learners to develop a large and varied vocabulary repertoire.

Key Features of the Lexical Approach:

1. Lexical Chunks: The lexical approach highlights the importance of teaching and learning vocabulary in chunks or collocations rather than isolated words. This enables learners to grasp the natural collocational patterns and usage of words, enhancing their fluency and accuracy.

2. Authentic Materials: The use of authentic materials, such as newspapers, magazines, and real-life texts, is a key feature of the lexical approach. By exposing learners to genuine language samples, they can explore vocabulary in context, understand idiomatic expressions, and acquire language patterns that reflect real-world usage.

3. Focus on Meaning: The lexical approach places a strong emphasis on meaning rather than form. This means that learners are encouraged to understand and use vocabulary in context, focusing on the communicative value of words and phrases rather than their grammatical structure.

4. Language Awareness: The lexical approach promotes language awareness by encouraging learners to analyze and explore the language they encounter. This includes raising awareness of word families, collocations, synonyms, and antonyms, enabling learners to make connections and expand their lexical knowledge.

Benefits of the Lexical Approach:

1. Enhanced Communication Skills: By focusing on vocabulary as the building blocks of communication, the lexical approach helps learners develop their speaking and writing skills. They become more fluent and accurate in expressing themselves, as they can draw upon a wider range of vocabulary to convey their thoughts and ideas.

2. Improved Listening and Reading Comprehension: Through exposure to authentic materials, learners using the lexical approach develop

better listening and reading comprehension skills. They are better equipped to understand idiomatic expressions, recognize collocations, and decipher meaning from context.

3. Increased Fluency: The lexical approach encourages learners to develop fluency by highlighting the importance of using chunks of language. Learners build their speaking and writing fluency by employing ready-made phrases and expressions, which helps them sound more natural and native-like.

4. Enhanced Vocabulary Retention: By focusing on vocabulary in meaningful contexts, the lexical approach promotes vocabulary retention. Learners are more likely to remember words and phrases when they encounter them in authentic situations, rather than through rote memorization.

The lexical approach offers a fresh perspective on language teaching and learning by placing vocabulary at the forefront. By emphasizing the importance of words and phrases in communication, this approach helps learners develop a more natural and authentic command of the language. Through the use of authentic materials, a focus on meaning, and an emphasis on language awareness, the lexical approach provides a comprehensive and effective method for language acquisition. By incorporating the principles and features of the lexical approach into language teaching, educators can empower learners to become competent and confident users of the target language.

Engage, Study and Activate

Enhancing Language Learning Effectiveness

In the field of language teaching, various methods and approaches have emerged over the years, each aiming to enhance the effectiveness of language learning. One such method that has gained popularity and recognition is the ESA (Engage, Study, Activate) teaching method. This comprehensive approach provides a structured framework for teachers to create engaging and interactive language lessons that cater to the diverse needs of learners. In this article, we will explore the ESA teaching method, its key components, and how it fosters effective language acquisition.

Engage:

The first stage of the ESA teaching method is the "Engage" phase. This stage aims to capture students' attention and motivate them to participate actively in the lesson. Teachers employ various techniques such as discussions, games, videos, or real-life examples to generate interest and curiosity among learners. The goal is to create a positive and enjoyable learning environment that stimulates students' engagement and promotes language use.

During the Engage stage, teachers introduce the topic or language point through a warm-up activity that encourages students to share their ideas and opinions. This initial interaction not only helps to activate prior knowledge but also establishes a connection between the students and the topic, making it relevant and meaningful to their lives.

Study:

The second phase of the ESA method is the "Study" stage. In this stage, the focus shifts towards structured language learning. Teachers provide explicit instruction on the language target, whether it be grammar, vocabulary, pronunciation, or any other language skill. This stage often involves the use of textbooks, worksheets, multimedia resources, or teacher-led explanations to present and practice the language point.

To ensure effective learning, teachers employ various teaching techniques, such as guided discovery, concept checking questions, and controlled practice exercises. Through these activities, students are guided to understand the language rules, patterns, and usage, fostering comprehension and fluency.

Activate:

The final stage of the ESA method is the "Activate" stage. At this point, learners are encouraged to apply the language they have learned in meaningful and authentic contexts. The Activate stage is characterized by interactive and communicative activities that promote fluency, creativity, and critical thinking. Students engage in pair or group work, discussions, role-plays, debates, or even project-based tasks, where they actively use the language to express their ideas, opinions, and experiences.

The Activate stage encourages students to take ownership of their learning and develop their language skills in a more independent and autonomous manner. It provides them with opportunities to use the language in real-life situations, fostering confidence and promoting a deeper understanding of the language's purpose and functionality.

Benefits of the ESA Teaching Method:

1. Engaging and Interactive Learning: The ESA method ensures that language lessons are dynamic, interactive, and student-centered. It enables teachers to create a positive and motivating learning environment that promotes active participation and engagement.

2. Contextualized Language Use: By connecting the language to real-life situations and experiences, the ESA method makes language learning more relevant and meaningful for learners. This approach enhances students' ability to apply the language in practical contexts, leading to better language acquisition.

3. Balanced Skills Development: The ESA method emphasizes all language skills - listening, speaking, reading, and writing. By incorporating a variety of activities and practice opportunities, it helps learners develop a well-rounded proficiency in the target language.

4. Personalization and Differentiation: The ESA method recognizes the diverse needs and learning styles of individual students. Teachers can adapt and personalize activities to cater to different levels, interests, and learning preferences, ensuring that every student benefits from the learning experience.

The ESA teaching method provides a comprehensive and structured framework for language teachers to deliver effective and engaging lessons. By incorporating the Engage, Study, and Activate stages, this method facilitates a holistic approach to language learning, fostering comprehension, fluency, and confidence among students. With its emphasis on student engagement, interactive learning, and contextualized language use, the ESA method proves to be an invaluable tool for language educators seeking to enhance the effectiveness of their teaching.

Chapter 4

Classroom Management

Classroom Management

Classroom management is at the heart of effective teaching and learning. It refers to the strategies and techniques employed by educators to create a positive and engaging learning environment that maximizes student learning and minimizes disruptions. A well-managed classroom not only enhances student achievement but also cultivates essential life skills such as responsibility, self-discipline, and respect. This comprehensive article will delve into various aspects of classroom management, providing educators with a toolbox of strategies to ensure a productive and harmonious learning experience for all students.

I. Establishing Clear Expectations and Rules:

One of the fundamental pillars of effective classroom management is setting clear expectations and establishing rules. By explicitly outlining behavioral expectations, academic standards, and classroom procedures, educators create a structured environment where students understand what is expected of them. This promotes a sense of safety, consistency, and predictability, enabling students to focus on learning while minimizing disruptive behaviors.

II. Building Positive Relationships:

Developing positive relationships with students is essential for effective classroom management. When students feel valued, respected, and supported, they are more likely to be engaged and motivated. Building rapport through active listening, empathy, and open communication fosters a positive classroom climate conducive to learning. Moreover, teachers who show genuine interest in their students' well-being and interests create a sense of belonging and trust, leading to improved behavior and cooperation.

III. Implementing Differentiated Instruction:

Recognizing that students have diverse learning needs and styles is crucial for successful classroom management. Employing differentiated instruction allows teachers to tailor their lessons to accommodate different learning preferences, abilities, and interests. By providing varied instructional approaches, materials, and assessments, educators can engage all students, maintain their interest, and prevent disruptive behaviors resulting from boredom or frustration.

IV. Effective Classroom Organization and Layout:

Proper classroom organization and layout play a pivotal role in promoting a conducive learning environment. A well-organized classroom includes designated spaces for specific activities, such as reading corners, workstations, and collaborative areas. Clear signage, labeled materials, and accessible resources enhance students' independence and minimize distractions. Additionally, an ergonomic and clutter-free classroom layout facilitates smooth movement, promotes teacher-student interaction, and ensures student safety.

V. Implementing Engaging Instructional Strategies:

Engaging instructional strategies are essential for capturing students' attention and maintaining their active participation. By incorporating varied teaching methods, such as hands-on activities, group work, technology integration, and real-world connections, educators can make learning relevant and exciting. Engaged students are less likely to exhibit disruptive behaviors, as they feel connected to the content and are actively involved in the learning process.

VI. Proactive Behavior Management:

Prevention is key to effective classroom management. Teachers can implement proactive behavior management strategies to minimize disruptions before they occur. These strategies may include establishing routines, providing clear directions, offering choices, and using positive reinforcement. By addressing potential triggers and proactively managing student behavior, educators create an environment that encourages positive interactions and reduces the need for disciplinary actions.

VII. Consistent Discipline and Consequences:

Although prevention is crucial, there will still be occasions when discipline is necessary. Consistency in disciplinary procedures and consequences is vital to maintain a well-managed classroom. By establishing a fair and transparent system that is consistently applied, students gain a clear understanding of the consequences of their actions. However, it is equally important to emphasize restorative rather than punitive approaches, focusing on learning from mistakes and fostering growth.

VIII. Collaboration with Parents and Guardians:

Collaboration between teachers and parents/guardians is an essential component of effective classroom management. Regular communication, whether through parent-teacher conferences, newsletters, or digital platforms, ensures that parents are aware of classroom expectations, student progress, and any concerns that may arise. Involving parents in the educational process fosters a partnership that supports students' development, reinforces classroom expectations, and promotes consistent behavior management across home and school environments.

Classroom management is a multifaceted skill that requires a combination of effective strategies, strong relationships, and a commitment to ongoing professional growth. By setting clear expectations, building positive relationships, implementing differentiated instruction, organizing the classroom effectively, engaging students with varied instructional strategies, employing proactive behavior management techniques, maintaining consistent discipline, and collaborating with parents, educators can create an optimal learning environment where students thrive academically and personally.

Harnessing the Power of Eye Contact in the English Teaching Classroom

In the realm of language teaching, effective communication is key, and one powerful tool that often goes overlooked is eye contact. Eye contact can greatly enhance the English teaching experience, as it helps foster engagement, connection, and understanding between teachers and students. In this article, we will explore how eye contact can be used to create an immersive and stimulating environment within an English teaching classroom.

1. Establishing Rapport:
Eye contact plays a crucial role in establishing rapport, building trust, and developing a positive relationship between teachers and students. By maintaining eye contact, teachers convey openness, attentiveness, and approachability, which encourages students to feel comfortable and confident in their learning environment. This initial connection lays the foundation for effective teaching and learning.

2. Enhancing Comprehension:
When teachers make eye contact with individual students or the entire

class, it helps to reinforce important information and increase comprehension. By looking directly at students, teachers can gauge their level of understanding, identify confusion, and adjust their teaching strategies accordingly. Additionally, eye contact allows students to feel acknowledged and encourages active participation, as they know they are being heard and valued.

3. Nonverbal Communication:
Eye contact is a powerful nonverbal communication tool that can be used to convey different meanings and emotions. Teachers can utilize eye contact to express encouragement, approval, or even provide gentle redirection. By using eye contact effectively, teachers can convey enthusiasm, empathy, and support, thereby creating a positive and motivating learning atmosphere.

4. Managing Classroom Dynamics:
Eye contact can be an invaluable tool for managing classroom dynamics and behavior. By establishing eye contact with disruptive or disengaged students, teachers can subtly communicate their expectations and redirect their attention back to the lesson. This non-verbal cue can help maintain discipline without disrupting the flow of the class and allows teachers to address issues discreetly and effectively.

5. Encouraging Active Listening:
Incorporating eye contact into classroom activities encourages students to actively listen and engage with the lesson. When students know that the teacher may make eye contact with them at any moment, they are more likely to pay attention, ask questions, and participate in discussions. Eye contact also helps create a sense of accountability, as students know they are being observed, which promotes a culture of active learning.

6. Fostering Cultural Understanding:
In an English teaching classroom, students often come from diverse

cultural backgrounds. Eye contact can be particularly useful in bridging cultural differences, as its interpretation may vary across cultures. By using eye contact appropriately and respectfully, teachers can promote cross-cultural understanding and sensitivity, making students comfortable and appreciated, irrespective of their cultural norms.

Eye contact is a powerful and often underestimated tool in the English teaching classroom. By utilizing its potential, teachers can establish rapport, enhance comprehension, facilitate nonverbal communication, manage classroom dynamics, encourage active listening, and foster cultural understanding. By incorporating eye contact into their teaching strategies, educators can create an immersive, engaging, and supportive environment that promotes effective language learning and student development. So, let's not underestimate the power of eye contact in the English teaching classroom and harness its potential to inspire and empower our students.

The Power of Gestures in the Classroom

In the realm of language acquisition, effective communication is key. English language teaching classrooms often strive to create an immersive and engaging environment for learners. One powerful tool that can significantly enhance the learning experience is the use of gestures. Incorporating gestures into English teaching not only helps to bridge communication gaps but also aids in comprehension, memory retention, and learner engagement. This comprehensive article aims to explore the various ways in which gestures can be effectively utilized in the English teaching classroom.

1. Non-verbal Communication:
Gestures serve as a universal language that can effortlessly convey meaning, regardless of the learner's linguistic background. Non-verbal cues, such as hand movements, facial expressions, and body language, can help clarify instructions, demonstrate vocabulary, and express emotions. These gestures create a visual context, making it easier for learners to understand and connect with the language being taught.

2. Vocabulary and Concept Reinforcement:
Gestures play a significant role in reinforcing vocabulary and concepts. When teaching new words or phrases, educators can use accompanying

gestures to illustrate their meanings. For example, when teaching the word "run," teachers can simulate the action of running, emphasizing the physical movement. This association between the gesture and the word helps learners retain the information more effectively, as it creates a multisensory learning experience.

3. Grammar and Sentence Structure:
Gestures can also be employed to teach grammar and sentence structure. For instance, when teaching prepositions, teachers can use gestures to demonstrate the relationship between objects in space. A simple hand gesture can effectively convey concepts such as "above," "below," "in front of," or "behind." This interactive approach not only aids comprehension but also encourages learners to actively participate in the learning process.

4. Storytelling and Role Play:
Gestures are particularly valuable when engaging learners in storytelling and role play activities. By incorporating gestures, teachers can bring stories to life, making them more captivating and relatable. Learners can actively participate by mimicking the gestures, enhancing their understanding of the narrative and improving their own storytelling skills. Role play activities benefit from gestures as well, as learners can use them to communicate effectively and express emotions while acting out different scenarios.

5. Classroom Management and Instructions:
Gestures can be instrumental in maintaining discipline and facilitating effective classroom management. Educators can use specific gestures to signal transitions, gain attention, or indicate behavioral expectations. For example, raising a finger to the lips can signify the need for silence or attentiveness. These non-verbal cues help minimize disruptions and create a harmonious learning environment.

6. Cultural Understanding:

Gestures can also aid in cultural understanding, especially in English teaching classrooms that have learners from diverse cultural backgrounds. By incorporating gestures from different cultures, teachers can promote cultural awareness and appreciation. Students can learn about the meaning and appropriate use of gestures, fostering respect and understanding for other cultures.

The incorporation of gestures in English teaching classrooms offers numerous benefits, ranging from improved comprehension and memory retention to enhanced engagement and cultural understanding. By utilizing gestures, educators can create a dynamic learning environment that caters to the diverse needs of learners. It is essential for teachers to explore and experiment with various gestures and find the most effective ways to integrate them into their teaching practices. Ultimately, gestures provide a powerful tool for English language educators to facilitate effective communication and create an immersive and engaging learning experience.

Harnessing the Power of the Teacher's Voice in the English Teaching Classroom

In the realm of language education, the teacher's voice plays a vital role in creating a conducive learning environment and facilitating effective communication. A teacher's voice can profoundly impact students' language acquisition, motivation, and engagement. This article delves into the various ways in which teachers can utilize their voice to maximize learning outcomes in an English teaching classroom.

1. Model Pronunciation and Fluency:
One of the primary functions of the teacher's voice is to serve as a model for correct pronunciation and fluent speech. By enunciating words clearly and articulating sounds accurately, teachers can help students develop their listening and speaking skills. Teachers should emphasize proper stress, intonation, and rhythm to improve students' overall oral proficiency.

2. Provide Clear Instructions:
A teacher's voice should be clear, concise, and well-paced when delivering instructions. By using appropriate volume and tone, teachers can

effectively convey the objectives and tasks to students. Clear instructions enhance understanding, minimize confusion, and promote better engagement with the lesson content.

3. Create a Positive Classroom Atmosphere:
The tone of a teacher's voice greatly influences the classroom atmosphere. A warm, friendly, and encouraging voice can create a positive learning environment where students feel comfortable expressing themselves. Varying the tone to match the content and context can also make the classroom more engaging and interesting for learners.

4. Utilize Voice Modulation for Emphasis:
A teacher's voice can be used to emphasize key points, important vocabulary, or specific language structures. By adjusting volume, pitch, and pace, teachers can draw attention to specific aspects of the lesson, helping students focus on and remember crucial information. This technique enhances comprehension and retention of language concepts.

5. Engage and Motivate Students:
A teacher's voice can serve as a catalyst for student engagement and motivation. By using an enthusiastic and passionate tone, teachers can convey their own excitement for the subject matter, which can be contagious. Students are more likely to be engaged and motivated when they sense the teacher's genuine interest and enthusiasm.

6. Encourage Active Participation:
The teacher's voice can be employed to encourage students to actively participate in class discussions and activities. By using open-ended questions, intonation, and encouraging language, teachers can create a safe and supportive environment for students to express their thoughts and ideas. This fosters critical thinking, fluency development, and confidence in using English.

7. Provide Feedback and Correction:

When giving feedback and correction, a teacher's voice should be constructive and positive. Using a supportive and encouraging tone helps students feel comfortable receiving feedback, enabling them to understand and correct their language errors effectively. Teachers should also employ intonation and stress patterns to highlight specific areas that need improvement, guiding students towards linguistic accuracy.

8. Introduce Authentic Materials:
The teacher's voice can be used to introduce authentic materials, such as videos, audio recordings, or interviews. By adding narration or commentary, teachers can guide students' understanding and interpretation of these materials. The teacher's voice acts as a bridge between the authentic language input and the students' comprehension.

The teacher's voice is a powerful tool in the English teaching classroom. By employing various techniques, such as modeling pronunciation, providing clear instructions, creating a positive atmosphere, and engaging students, teachers can enhance language acquisition and promote effective communication. The teacher's voice should be seen as a resourceful instrument that, when used effectively, can significantly impact students' learning experiences and outcomes.

Why should we use Students' Names in an English Language Class?

In any educational setting, creating a positive and engaging learning environment is essential to foster student growth and success. A simple yet powerful tool that can contribute to this environment is the use of students' names. Recognizing and using students' names in an English language class can have numerous benefits, ranging from building rapport and enhancing motivation to improving classroom management and facilitating effective communication. This article explores the various advantages of incorporating students' names and provides practical tips for teachers to implement this practice effectively.

1. Establishing Rapport and Building Relationships:
Using students' names creates a sense of belonging and validates their individual identities within the classroom. By addressing them by their names, teachers foster a positive and inclusive environment that promotes trust, respect, and rapport. This personalized approach allows students to feel seen, heard, and valued, ultimately strengthening the teacher-student relationship and encouraging students to actively participate in classroom activities.

2. Enhancing Motivation and Engagement:

When students' names are frequently used in class, they feel more connected and invested in their learning. This personalized attention boosts their self-esteem and motivation, as they perceive themselves as active participants rather than mere spectators. It fosters a sense of ownership over their progress and encourages them to take risks, engage in discussions, and contribute their unique perspectives.

3. Improving Classroom Management:

Addressing students by their names can significantly enhance classroom management. By using their names, teachers can gain students' attention more effectively, avoiding the need for repeated instructions or disruptive behavior. Additionally, it facilitates individualized feedback, allowing teachers to provide specific guidance and praise, which positively impacts student behavior and encourages a conducive learning environment.

4. Facilitating Effective Communication:

Using students' names in class promotes effective communication by ensuring clarity and precision. In language learning, pronunciation and phonetics play a crucial role. By repeatedly saying their names correctly and encouraging correct pronunciation from others, teachers help students improve their language skills. Furthermore, students become more comfortable with speaking up, asking questions, and seeking clarification, as they feel a stronger sense of connection with their teacher and peers.

Practical Tips for Using Students' Names:

a. Learn and Practice Pronunciation: Take time to familiarize yourself with the correct pronunciation of each student's name. Practice saying their names aloud and seek assistance from students if necessary. Remember that a student's name is an integral part of their identity, and mispronouncing it can be disrespectful.

b. Use Names Regularly: Incorporate students' names into your teaching routine. Greet them individually at the beginning of the class, use their names when asking questions or giving instructions, and address them directly during discussions or group work.

c. Reinforce Positive Behavior: Use students' names when providing positive reinforcement or praising their achievements. This personal touch reinforces their efforts and encourages continued growth.

d. Encourage Peer Interactions: Promote a classroom culture where students use each other's names when collaborating, discussing ideas, or providing feedback. This practice encourages inclusivity, respect, and active engagement among peers.

e. Be Mindful of Cultural Sensitivities: Recognize and respect cultural norms and sensitivities surrounding names. Some students may prefer to use a nickname or have a specific cultural practice surrounding their name. Be open to accommodating their preferences and ensure an inclusive environment for all.

The use of students' names in an English language class is a simple yet powerful tool that has numerous benefits. By establishing rapport, enhancing motivation, improving classroom management, and facilitating effective communication, teachers can create an inclusive and engaging learning environment. Implementing the practical tips outlined in this article can help teachers harness the full potential of using students' names, leading to improved student outcomes and a more enjoyable learning experience for all.

Grouping Students in English Language Classes: Advantages and Disadvantages

Grouping students in English language classes is a common practice employed by educators to enhance language learning. By organizing students into smaller groups, teachers can provide targeted instruction, encourage peer interaction, and foster a collaborative learning environment. However, this approach also has its drawbacks. In this article, we will explore the advantages and disadvantages of grouping students in English language classes, allowing educators to make informed decisions about its implementation.

Advantages of Grouping Students:

1. Increased Opportunity for Active Learning:
Group work in English language classes promotes active learning, as students are actively engaged in discussions, problem-solving, and co-operative activities. This approach encourages students to use the language in practical contexts, enhancing their speaking, listening, reading, and writing skills.

2. Enhanced Language Production:
Working in groups encourages students to practice speaking and express their thoughts and opinions in English. This increased language production helps students overcome their fear of making mistakes and builds their confidence in using the language.

3. Peer Collaboration and Support:
Grouping students enables peer collaboration and support, which can be invaluable in language learning. Through peer interaction, students can clarify doubts, exchange ideas, and learn from each other's strengths. This collaborative approach fosters a sense of community and mutual support among students.

4. Diverse Perspectives and Cultural Understanding:
Grouping students in English language classes allows for the inclusion of diverse perspectives and backgrounds. Interaction among students from different cultures and language backgrounds promotes cultural understanding, empathy, and appreciation for diversity, which are essential in today's globalized world.

5. Efficient Use of Resources:
In larger classes, grouping students optimizes the use of resources, such as time, teaching materials, and classroom space. With smaller groups, teachers can provide more personalized attention, monitor individual progress, and tailor instruction to meet the specific needs of each group.

Disadvantages of Grouping Students:

1. Unequal Group Dynamics:
Grouping students may result in uneven dynamics within the groups. Some groups may have dominant members who overshadow others, leading to reduced participation and unequal distribution of workload. Teachers must carefully manage group dynamics to ensure everyone has an equal opportunity to contribute and learn.

2. Potential for Social Loafing:
In certain group settings, the phenomenon of social loafing may occur, where some students may rely on their peers to complete tasks without actively participating. This can hamper individual learning and hinder the overall progress of the group. Teachers need to implement strategies to ensure active participation from all group members.

3. Limited Individual Attention:
Grouping students can limit the individual attention that teachers can provide. While it may be beneficial for some students to work collaboratively, others may require more one-on-one support. Teachers must strike a balance between group work and individual attention to cater to the diverse needs of students.

4. Conflict and Disagreements:
Working in groups can sometimes lead to conflicts and disagreements among students, especially when different opinions and perspectives are involved. Teachers must guide students in developing effective communication and conflict resolution skills to ensure a harmonious learning environment.

5. Varied Learning Paces:
Students within a group may have different learning paces and language proficiency levels. This can pose a challenge in terms of delivering instruction at an appropriate pace that suits everyone. Teachers must differentiate instruction within the groups, providing additional support or challenging tasks as needed.

Grouping students in English language classes offers numerous advantages, including increased active learning, enhanced language production, peer collaboration, cultural understanding, and efficient resource utilization. However, educators must also be mindful of the potential disadvantages, such as uneven group dynamics, social loafing, limited individual attention, conflicts, and varied learning paces. By understanding the pros and cons, teachers can effectively plan and implement group work strategies to maximize the benefits and mitigate the drawbacks, ultimately fostering a conducive learning environment for all students.

Exploring the Advantages and Disadvantages of Pair Work in English Language Classes

Pair work has become a widely adopted teaching approach in English language classes. This method involves students working in pairs or small groups to complete various language learning tasks. While pair work can offer several advantages, it also has its fair share of drawbacks. In this article, we will delve into the benefits and disadvantages of implementing pair work in English language classrooms.

Advantages of Pair Work:

1. Increased Student Engagement:
Pair work encourages active participation and engagement from each student. It provides an opportunity for students to take ownership of their learning and actively practice their language skills. When students work together, they are more likely to feel motivated and inspired to contribute, resulting in a more dynamic and interactive classroom environment.

2. Enhanced Communication Skills:

Pair work enables students to practice their speaking and listening skills in a safe and non-threatening environment. By engaging in conversations with their peers, students can develop their fluency, pronunciation, and vocabulary. It also fosters better understanding of different accents and communication styles, thus improving overall communication skills.

3. Collaborative Learning:
Pair work fosters a sense of collaboration and teamwork among students. It encourages students to share ideas, discuss concepts, and solve problems together. Through this process, students develop important skills such as critical thinking, negotiation, and cooperation, which are vital not only in language learning but also in real-life situations.

4. Increased Speaking Time:
In traditional classroom settings, students often have limited opportunities to speak due to time constraints. Pair work allows for increased speaking time as students engage in meaningful conversations with their partners. This extra practice helps to build confidence in speaking English, allowing students to develop fluency and accuracy at a faster pace.

5. Personalized Learning:
Pair work provides an opportunity for individualized attention within a group setting. Students can discuss their strengths and weaknesses with their partners, providing constructive feedback and support. This personalized approach allows students to focus on their specific language needs and progress at their own pace.

Disadvantages of Pair Work:

1. Unequal Participation:
One of the challenges of pair work is ensuring equal participation from both students. In some cases, one student may dominate the conversation while the other remains passive. This can hinder the progress and

learning of the less active student, leading to a potential imbalance in language development.

2. Limited Feedback:
While pair work allows for peer feedback, it may not always be accurate or comprehensive. Students may lack the necessary language knowledge or teaching skills to provide constructive feedback. In such cases, important mistakes may go unnoticed, resulting in the reinforcement of incorrect language usage.

3. Lack of Teacher Control:
During pair work activities, the teacher has less control over the classroom dynamic. This can lead to off-task behavior, noise, or distractions. It requires careful monitoring and management by the teacher to ensure that students remain focused and on track with their learning objectives.

4. Reduced Exposure to Different Language Models:
In pair work, students primarily interact with their partners, limiting exposure to different accents, vocabulary, and communication styles. This lack of exposure may hinder the development of their listening and comprehension skills, as they are not exposed to a wide range of language models.

5. Limited Interaction Opportunities:
Pair work activities often restrict interactions to a single partner, limiting opportunities for students to engage with a variety of classmates. This may hinder the development of social and interpersonal skills, as students may miss out on the chance to collaborate with different personalities and cultural backgrounds.

Pair work is a valuable teaching approach in English language classrooms, offering numerous advantages such as increased student engagement, enhanced communication skills, and collaborative learning.

However, it is important to acknowledge and address the potential drawbacks, including unequal participation, limited feedback, and reduced exposure to diverse language models. By carefully designing and implementing pair work activities, teachers can maximize the benefits while minimizing the disadvantages, creating a balanced and effective learning environment for their students.

Exploring Effective Seating Arrangements in the English Language Classroom

Creating a conducive learning environment is crucial for student engagement and academic success in any classroom. The seating arrangement plays a vital role in enhancing student interaction, participation, and collaboration. In an English language class, where effective communication is paramount, it becomes even more important to consider appropriate seating arrangements. In this article, we will delve into the various seating arrangement strategies, their benefits, and the factors to consider when implementing them.

1. Traditional Rows Seating:
The traditional rows seating is the most common seating arrangement, with students sitting in straight rows facing the front of the classroom. This arrangement is useful for teacher-centered activities, such as lectures or presentations. It promotes discipline and allows students to focus on the teacher's instruction. However, it can hinder student interaction and collaboration.

2. U-Shaped Seating:

The U-shaped seating arrangement is ideal for engaging students in discussions, debates, or group activities. By having students face each other, it encourages interaction and peer-to-peer learning. In an English language class, this arrangement promotes communication skills, active listening, and empathy. The teacher can easily move around the U-shape, providing individual attention to students.

3. Clusters and Pods Seating:

Clusters and pods seating arrangements involve placing desks or tables together in small groups or clusters. This arrangement fosters collaboration, teamwork, and communication among students. In an English language class, it encourages student-to-student interaction, allowing for group work, pair discussions, and cooperative learning. Students can practice English in a more casual and relaxed setting, building their confidence.

4. Circle Seating:

The circle seating arrangement is highly effective for developing a sense of equality and inclusivity in the English language classroom. By bringing everyone into a circle, every student can see and hear one another clearly. This arrangement promotes open discussions, encourages active participation, and helps build a supportive learning community. In terms of language learning, students have equal opportunities to express their thoughts, opinions, and questions.

Factors to Consider:

When implementing seating arrangements, several factors should be considered:

a. Classroom Size and Layout: The physical attributes of the classroom, such as size and shape, determine the feasibility of certain seating arrangements. It is essential to ensure that all students have adequate space to move around comfortably.

b. Teaching Style and Lesson Objectives: The choice of seating arrangement should align with the teaching style and lesson objectives. For example, if the lesson requires a lecture format, traditional rows seating may be suitable. On the other hand, if the objective is to promote conversation skills, a U-shaped or circle seating arrangement would be more appropriate.

c. Student Preferences and Dynamics: Understanding student preferences, personalities, and dynamics can help in grouping students effectively. A balanced mix of personalities within groups can encourage cooperation and avoid potential conflicts.

d. Classroom Management: The chosen seating arrangement should be practical for classroom management. The teacher should be able to easily monitor student activities, provide timely feedback, and address any concerns.

Seating arrangements in an English language class can greatly impact student engagement, communication skills, and overall learning outcomes. It is essential for teachers to consider various seating strategies and select the most appropriate arrangement based on the lesson objectives, classroom dynamics, and student preferences. By creating an environment that fosters interaction, collaboration, and active learning, teachers can maximize the language learning potential of their students.

The Importance of Teacher's Sitting and Standing Positions in an English Language Class

In an English language class, the teacher's posture and position play a crucial role in creating an effective learning environment. The way a teacher sits or stands can impact students' engagement, comprehension, and overall learning experience. This article will delve into the significance of a teacher's sitting and standing positions, highlighting the implications for student interaction, classroom management, and effective communication.

1. Establishing Authority and Classroom Management:

A teacher's standing position often subconsciously communicates their authority and control over the class. By standing tall and maintaining an upright posture, the teacher sets a professional tone in the classroom, encouraging students to respect and follow their lead. Conversely, sitting down might create a more relaxed atmosphere, potentially resulting in a lack of control or attention from students. However, a teacher must strike a balance between being approachable and maintaining discipline, adapting their position accordingly based on the situation.

2. Visual Accessibility and Eye Contact:

When a teacher stands, they naturally have better visibility of the entire classroom, making it easier to monitor student behavior, engagement, and understanding. This vantage point allows teachers to detect signs of confusion, provide individual attention, or redirect students back on track. Moreover, maintaining eye contact with students fosters a sense of connection and encourages active participation. By ensuring eye contact with a diverse range of students, regardless of their location in the classroom, the teacher can make the learning experience more inclusive and engaging for all.

3. Facilitating Classroom Interaction:

An English language class thrives on student participation and group activities. In these scenarios, a teacher's ability to move around the classroom becomes crucial. By walking between desks or group circles, teachers can circulate freely, observe student interactions, provide feedback, and facilitate discussions. This mobility enhances student-teacher rapport and encourages collaborative learning. Furthermore, a teacher's active presence helps increase students' engagement levels, as they feel more accountable when the instructor is within proximity.

4. Adaptive Instruction and Personalized Support:

Certain classroom activities may require a teacher to use a multifunctional approach that involves sitting with students. For instance, during small-group or one-on-one discussions, sitting alongside students strengthens engagement, encourages open dialogue, and promotes a less hierarchical atmosphere. It fosters a sense of trust and rapport between the teacher and students, creating an environment conducive to personalized support and guidance.

5. Modeling Listening and Speaking Skills:

An English language class places significant emphasis on communication skills. When the teacher takes a seat during discussions, students witness a demonstration of attentive listening. It encourages them to follow suit, actively listening to their peers with respect and interest. By adopting an active listening stance, the teacher models proper turn-taking and conversational etiquette, facilitating an engaging learning environment.

The teacher's sitting and standing positions in an English language class have a substantial impact on the overall learning experience. By understanding the implications of their positions, teachers can effectively manage the classroom, ensure visual accessibility, foster classroom interaction, and provide personalized support. Striking a balance between sitting and standing allows teachers to adapt to different activities, maximize student engagement, and facilitate effective communication. Ultimately, a teacher's conscious effort in this regard can greatly enhance the quality of English language instruction and the students' overall learning journey.

Balancing Teacher Talking Time and Student Talking Time in English Language Classes

In English language classes, finding the optimal balance between teacher talking time (TTT) and student talking time (STT) is crucial for effective language learning. While teachers play a vital role in sharing knowledge and providing guidance, empowering students to actively participate and engage in conversations is equally essential. This article aims to explore the importance of TTT and STT, the challenges in achieving a balance, and strategies to facilitate effective language learning in the classroom.

The Significance of Teacher Talking Time (TTT):

1. Knowledge Dissemination: Teachers are experts in the English language and play a crucial role in delivering content and explanations. Their extensive linguistic competence helps students to acquire vocabulary, grammar rules, and pronunciation patterns.

2. Guided Instruction: Teachers set the tone for the class, establish learning goals, and provide models for correct language usage. Through

TTT, teachers can impart important language skills and strategies necessary for effective communication.

3. Classroom Management: TTT helps maintain order and discipline as teachers provide instructions, ask questions, and organize activities. It serves as a tool to guide students' attention and facilitate the learning process.

The Importance of Student Talking Time (STT):

1. Active Engagement: Allowing students ample opportunities to speak enhances their active participation and engagement in the learning process. STT fosters confidence, fluency, and spontaneous language production.

2. Error Correction and Feedback: Through STT, teachers can identify and correct students' language errors, providing guidance and feedback on pronunciation, grammar, vocabulary, and overall communication skills.

3. Collaborative Learning: STT promotes collaboration and a student-centered approach by encouraging peer-to-peer interaction. Students can practice expressing themselves, negotiate meaning, and foster a sense of community within the classroom.

Challenges in Achieving a Balance:

1. Teacher Dominance: Teachers, due to their expertise and role, can sometimes unintentionally monopolize class time, leading to limited STT. It is crucial for instructors to be aware of their own talking habits and ensure that students have equal opportunities to speak.

2. Time Constraints: Teachers often face time constraints when trying to cover a curriculum or meet specific learning objectives, and this can negatively impact STT. Striking a balance between covering content and allocating time for student interaction is therefore a challenge.

3. Student Language Proficiency: Varied language proficiency levels among students can affect STT. Less proficient students may feel hesitant to speak in front of the class, while more advanced students might dominate the conversation. Teachers must employ strategies to create an inclusive and supportive environment for all learners.

Strategies to Facilitate Effective Language Learning:

1. Clear Communication Expectations: Set clear goals for TTT and STT at the beginning of each lesson, emphasizing the importance of active student participation and balanced class interaction.

2. Structured Pair and Group Work: Encourage pair and group work activities to maximize STT. Assigning roles and tasks ensures equal participation and allows students to practice language skills in a supportive setting.

3. Use of Technology: Incorporate technology tools, such as online discussion forums, chat platforms, or video conferencing, to extend STT beyond classroom walls. These platforms offer additional opportunities for language practice and collaboration.

4. Error Correction Techniques: Adopt effective error correction strategies, such as providing feedback during or after speaking activities, and encouraging self-correction and peer correction. This approach maintains a balance between correcting errors and fostering an encouraging learning atmosphere.

5. Monitor and Adjust: Regularly monitor TTT and STT ratios during class and adjust accordingly. This promotes reflection and awareness, allowing teachers to create a balance that suits the needs of their students.

Achieving an optimal balance between TTT and STT in English language classrooms is a dynamic process that requires awareness, intentionality, and adaptability. Teachers should utilize their expertise while empowering students to actively engage in the learning process through ample STT opportunities. By striking this balance, educators create an environment where students feel supported, motivated, and equipped to become confident and proficient English language speakers.

4-11

Establishing Rapport

Establishing rapport is a crucial aspect of creating an environment conducive to effective teaching and learning. This holds particularly true in an English language class, where communication and language skills development are at the forefront. In this article, we will explore the importance of developing rapport, identify strategies to foster connections with students, and highlight the benefits of a strong teacher-student rapport in an English language classroom.

1. Understanding the Significance of Rapport:
Rapport refers to the harmonious connection and understanding between individuals. In a language learning context, rapport plays a crucial role in motivating students, enhancing their confidence, and encouraging their active participation. When students feel comfortable and respected, they are more likely to engage in meaningful conversations, take risks in expressing themselves, and ultimately make progress.

2. Creating a Positive Classroom Climate:
a. Greet students warmly: Begin each class session with a warm and genuine greeting. This simple gesture helps students feel acknowledged and valued, setting a positive tone for the entire lesson.

b. Establish classroom routines: Consistency in routines helps students feel secure and understand expectations. Share clear guidelines and rules and ensure they are applied consistently.

c. Use positive reinforcement: Offer regular praise and encouragement to acknowledge students' efforts and achievements. Celebrate their successes and provide constructive feedback to foster continuous improvement.

3. Getting to Know Students:

a. Build a personal connection: Take the time to learn about your students' interests, hobbies, and goals. Incorporate these aspects into discussions and lessons to make learning more relevant and engaging for them.

b. Conduct icebreaker activities: At the beginning of the course, organize icebreaker activities to help students get to know each other. This creates a sense of community and encourages interaction among classmates.

c. Individualize learning experiences: Tailor your teaching approach to accommodate students' needs and learning styles. This demonstrates your understanding of their unique abilities and fosters a sense of inclusivity.

4. Engaging in Effective Communication:

a. Active listening: Demonstrate active listening by paying attention to students' responses and asking follow-up questions. This shows that their thoughts and opinions are valued, encouraging deeper engagement.

b. Non-verbal communication: Be aware of your non-verbal cues, such as maintaining eye contact, smiling, and using open body language. These gestures help create an inclusive and supportive atmosphere.

c. Use humor and anecdotes: Incorporate humor and share personal anecdotes appropriately to create a relaxed and enjoyable learning environment. This can help ease tension and build rapport among students.

5. Encouraging Collaboration and Participation:

a. Group work activities: Design collaborative tasks that require students to work together, fostering teamwork and peer support. This allows students to learn from one another and builds a sense of camaraderie.

b. Active participation: Create opportunities for students to actively engage in class discussions, debates, presentations, and role-plays. Encourage them to express their opinions, ask questions, and engage in critical thinking.

Benefits of Building Rapport:

a. Increased motivation: When students feel connected to their teacher and classmates, they are more motivated to participate actively and engage in the learning process.

b. Enhanced learning outcomes: A strong rapport facilitates effective communication, leading to improved language skills development and comprehension.

c. Reduced anxiety: A positive classroom environment built on rapport helps alleviate anxiety and fear of making mistakes, promoting a safe space for language learning.

Establishing rapport in an English language class is crucial for fostering a supportive and engaging learning environment. By employing strategies such as creating a positive classroom climate, getting to know students, engaging in effective communication, and encouraging collaboration, teachers can build strong connections with their students. The benefits of fostering rapport in an English language class include increased motivation, enhanced learning outcomes, and reduced anxiety. Ultimately, a strong teacher-student rapport will promote an enjoyable and effective language learning experience for all.

Problem Behavior in English Language Classes: Causes, Impacts, and Strategies for Effective Classroom Management

Problem behavior in English language classes can significantly disrupt the learning process and hinder the progress of students. It is crucial for educators to understand the causes and impacts of such behavior, as well as develop effective strategies to ensure a conducive learning environment. This comprehensive article aims to explore the various aspects of problem behavior in English language classes and offer practical solutions for effective classroom management.

Understanding Problem Behavior:

Problem behavior encompasses a range of actions that divert attention away from the learning process, disrupt classroom dynamics, or create an unsupportive learning environment. Some common examples of problem behavior in English language classes include students not paying attention, being disruptive, talking out of turn, and engaging in disrespectful behavior towards peers or the teacher.

Causes of Problem Behavior:

Several factors contribute to problem behavior in English language classes. These can include:

1. Lack of engagement: Students may become disinterested in the subject matter, leading to lack of motivation and increased likelihood of disruptive behavior.

2. Difficulties in comprehension: Struggling to understand the content may frustrate students, leading to disruptive behavior to mask their struggles or seek attention.

3. Language barriers: Students with limited English proficiency may feel overwhelmed or embarrassed, leading to disengagement or disruptive behavior.

4. External factors: Personal issues at home, social pressures, or conflicts with peers can influence students' behavior in the classroom.

Impacts of Problem Behavior:

Problem behavior in English language classes can have detrimental effects on students, their peers, and the overall learning environment. These impacts include:

1. Reduced learning outcomes: Problem behavior disrupts the ability of students to concentrate and engage fully in the learning process, leading to diminished academic achievements.

2. Negative classroom atmosphere: Disruptive behavior can create a tense and unsupportive environment, affecting the confidence and participation of other students.

3. Teacher burnout: Consistently managing problem behavior can be emotionally draining for teachers, impacting their effectiveness and job satisfaction.

Strategies for Effective Classroom Management:

1. Set Clear Expectations:

Establishing clear expectations from the beginning is essential for preventing problem behavior. Clearly communicate and discuss the class rules, routines, and consequences with your students. By having shared expectations, students will understand what is required of them and what the consequences will be for not meeting these expectations.

2. Foster a Positive Relationship:

Developing a positive relationship with your students is key to effectively managing problem behavior. Get to know your students individually, show interest in their lives, and be approachable. Building a rapport will create a supportive environment where students feel comfortable discussing any issues they are facing.

3. Implement a Behavior Management Plan:

Create a behavior management plan that includes a range of strategies to address problem behavior. This plan may include:

a) Positive Reinforcement: Acknowledge and reward positive behavior with verbal praise, stickers, or small incentives. This will encourage students to repeat desirable behavior and promote a positive classroom culture.

b) Proximity and Non-Verbal Cues: Stand close to students who exhibit problem behavior to remind them of your presence and redirect their attention. Use non-verbal cues, such as eye contact or a raised eyebrow, to communicate your expectations without disrupting the class.

c) Verbal Corrections and Reminders: Address problem behavior directly and calmly. Use a private conversation if necessary to avoid embarrassing the student in front of their peers. Remind them of the class rules and the consequences of their actions.

d) Time-Out or Cooling-off Period: If problem behavior persists, consider implementing a brief time-out or cooling-off period where the student can reflect on their actions. This can be done in the classroom or a designated area outside, always ensuring their safety.

e) Logical Consequences: Apply logical consequences that are directly related to the problem behavior. For example, if a student continually interrupts others while speaking, they may need to wait for a designated time before participating in class discussions.

4. Active Engagement Strategies:

Implementing active engagement strategies can reduce boredom and prevent off-task behavior. Incorporate a variety of interactive activities that cater to different learning styles, such as group work, role-plays, games, multimedia resources, and hands-on tasks. By keeping the class lively and engaging, you're more likely to maintain students' attention and minimize problem behavior.

5. Restorative Practices:

Introduce restorative practices as a way to address problem behavior while fostering accountability and empathy. Restorative practices involve a dialogue between the student involved in the problem behavior, their peers, and the teacher. It provides an opportunity for reflection, understanding the impact of their behavior, and making amends with the affected parties.

6. Collaboration with Parents or Guardians:

Maintaining open and frequent communication with parents or guardians is crucial. Inform them about any instances of problem behavior and discuss possible solutions collaboratively. By involving the parents, you can gain a better understanding of the student's context, personal challenges, and create a united approach towards addressing problem behavior.

Responding to problem behavior in an English language class requires a multifaceted approach that involves setting clear expectations, fostering positive relationships, implementing a behavior management plan, utilizing active engagement strategies, adopting restorative practices, and collaborating with parents or guardians. By consistently applying these strategies, educators can create a positive and productive learning environment where students thrive, allowing for effective English language instruction and personal growth.

Chapter 5

Presenting and Practicing Language

5-1

Understanding English Vocabulary

Students should have a good understanding of English vocabulary items to effectively communicate and comprehend written and spoken English. Here are some important things students need to know about English vocabulary:

1. **Word Definitions**: Students should know the meanings of words. This includes understanding both the denotative (literal) and connotative (implied or suggested) meanings.

2. **Part of Speech**: Students should be able to identify whether a word is a noun, verb, adjective, adverb, etc. This helps in proper word usage.

3. **Pronunciation**: Knowing how to pronounce words correctly is crucial for effective communication. Use resources like dictionaries with audio or language learning apps to practice.

4. **Spelling**: Correct spelling is essential for writing and reading comprehension. Spelling mistakes can change the meaning of a word.

5. **Synonyms and Antonyms**: Students should be aware of words with similar meanings (synonyms) and opposite meanings (antonyms). This enriches their vocabulary and enables more precise expression.

6. **Contextual Usage**: Understanding how words are used in different contexts is vital. Some words have multiple meanings depending on the context in which they are used.

7. **Collocations**: Knowing which words tend to appear together in natural language usage is important. For example, we "make" a decision, not "do" a decision.

8. **Idioms and Phrasal Verbs**: English is rich in idiomatic expressions and phrasal verbs. Students should learn common ones to understand native speakers better.

9. **Word Families**: Recognizing word families, which consist of a base word and its derivations (e.g., happy, happiness, happily), helps students understand word formation.

10. **Word Origins (Etymology)**: Learning the origin of words can provide insights into their meanings and help in understanding related words in English and other languages.

11. **Word Frequency**: Some words are used more frequently than others in everyday conversation and writing. Students should focus on high-frequency words to improve their practical language skills.

12. **Register and Formality**: Understanding when and where to use formal or informal language is important. For example, "could you" is more formal than "can you."

13. **Cultural and Regional Variations**: English vocabulary can vary by region and culture. Students should be aware of these variations to navigate different English-speaking communities.

14. **Word Learning Strategies**: Developing effective strategies for learning new words, such as creating flashcards, using mnemonic devices, or keeping a vocabulary journal, can aid in retention.

15. **Vocabulary Assessment**: Regularly assessing and expanding vocabulary through quizzes, reading, and active practice is key to vocabulary development.

16. **Context Clues**: Learning how to use context clues in reading or listening to deduce the meaning of unfamiliar words is a valuable skill.

17. **Word Choice**: Understanding that selecting the right word for a particular context is crucial for effective communication.

18. **Wordplay and Figurative Language**: Being familiar with wordplay, metaphors, similes, and other figurative language devices can enhance language comprehension and creativity.

19. **Specialized Vocabulary**: Depending on their interests and goals, students may need to learn specialized vocabulary related to their field of study or career.

20. **Continuous Learning**: Vocabulary development is an ongoing process. Encourage students to continually expand their vocabulary throughout their lives.

Ultimately, a strong vocabulary is an essential component of language proficiency. It enhances reading comprehension, writing skills, and the ability to express oneself clearly and effectively in spoken and written communication.

A Sample Lesson Plan for Teaching Vocabulary

Subject: English Vocabulary Lesson
Level: Pre-intermediate
Duration: 60 minutes
Method: Engage, Study, and Activate (ESA)

Objective: By the end of this lesson, students will be able to expand their English vocabulary related to weather and use these words in context through engaging activities.

Materials:

1. Whiteboard and markers
2. Flashcards with weather-related vocabulary words (e.g., sunny, rainy, windy, cloudy, stormy, etc.)
3. Images representing different weather conditions
4. Worksheets with sentences related to weather
5. Computers or tablets with internet access (optional)
6. Audio recording of a weather forecast (optional)

Procedure:
1. Engage (15 minutes):

- Begin the lesson by showing images representing different weather conditions (sunny, rainy, windy, etc.) and asking students to describe what they see.
- Elicit vocabulary words related to weather from the students and write them on the board.
- Play a short audio recording of a weather forecast or show a weather report video (optional) and have a brief discussion about the weather conditions mentioned in the forecast.

2. Study (20 minutes):

- Introduce the flashcards with weather-related vocabulary words. Show each flashcard and pronounce the word clearly, having students repeat after you.
- Provide definitions, synonyms, and antonyms for each word. Write them on the board.
- Use the flashcards in various activities: a. Matching: Distribute the flashcards among students and have them find a partner with a matching weather condition (e.g., sunny and sunny, rainy and rainy). b. Sentence formation: In pairs or small groups, have students use the vocabulary words to create sentences related to weather. c. Fill in the blank: Provide sentences with missing words and have students fill in the blanks with the appropriate vocabulary words.

3. Activate (20 minutes):

- In this phase, students will apply their newly acquired vocabulary in context.
- Distribute worksheets with sentences related to weather, leaving some blanks where students need to insert the correct weather-related vocabulary word.
- Encourage students to work individually or in pairs to complete the worksheet.

- As a class, review and discuss the completed worksheets, ensuring that students are using the vocabulary words correctly.
- For advanced learners, you can have them create short weather reports in pairs or small groups. They can use the vocabulary words to describe the current weather conditions in a fictional location and present their reports to the class.

4. Closure (5 minutes):

- Summarize the key points of the lesson, emphasizing the new vocabulary words related to weather.
- Ask students to share one sentence they created using a weather-related vocabulary word.
- Assign homework, such as writing a short paragraph about their favorite weather and using at least three of the vocabulary words from the lesson.

Assessment: Assessment can be done informally during class discussions, activities, and the completion of worksheets. Additionally, you can assign homework or quizzes to gauge students' understanding and retention of the new vocabulary words.

Adaptations: For students with different learning needs, consider providing additional support or modifying activities as necessary. This may include providing visuals, using simpler vocabulary words, or allowing extra time for assignments.

5-3

English Language Functions

English language functions refer to the different purposes or intentions behind communication in the English language. These functions are used to convey meaning, exchange information, and interact with others effectively. They are essential for effective communication and are often categorized into various types. Here are some common English language functions:

- **Requesting:** This function is used to ask for something or make a polite or direct request. For example, "Could you pass the salt, please?" or "Can you help me with this?"

- **Apologizing:** Apologizing is used to express regret or say sorry for something you've done or failed to do. For instance, "I'm sorry for being late."

- **Offering:** When you want to provide help or offer something to someone, you use this function. For example, "Would you like some coffee?" or "I can give you a ride."

- **Accepting/Declining:** These functions involve either agreeing to something or refusing an offer or request. For example, "I'd love to come to the party" (accepting) or "I'm sorry, but I can't make it" (declining).

- **Giving/Receiving Information:** You use this function to share or receive information. For instance, "The meeting is at 2 PM" (giving information) or "I heard it will rain tomorrow" (receiving information).

- **Agreeing/Disagreeing:** When you want to express your agreement or disagreement with someone's statement or idea, you use this function. For example, "I completely agree with you" (agreeing) or "I'm afraid I don't agree" (disagreeing).

- **Expressing Opinions:** This function involves sharing your thoughts, feelings, or beliefs about a topic. For example, "In my opinion, this movie is fantastic."

- **Suggesting:** When you propose an idea, solution, or course of action, you are using this function. For instance, "How about we go for a walk?" or "You could try calling customer support."

- **Complimenting:** Compliments are used to express admiration or praise for someone or something. For example, "You look beautiful in that dress" or "This meal is delicious."

- **Complaining:** To express dissatisfaction or raise an issue, you use this function. For instance, "The service here is terrible" or "I don't like the way he treats me."

- **Congratulating:** Congratulating is used to express joy or pleasure at someone's achievement or good news. For example, "Congratulations on your promotion!"

- **Asking for Permission:** When you want to get approval or consent for something, you use this function. For instance, "May I borrow your pen?"

- **Giving Advice:** To offer suggestions or recommendations to someone, you use this function. For example, "You should see a doctor if you're feeling sick."

- **Describing:** Describing involves providing details about a person, place, object, or event. For example, "The Eiffel Tower is a tall, iron structure located in Paris."

These language functions help people communicate effectively in various situations and contexts, allowing them to express themselves, interact with others, and convey their intentions clearly. They are an essential part of language learning and proficiency.

5-4

Why is it important to teach English Language Functions?

Teaching English Language Functions is important for several reasons:

- **Effective Communication**: Language functions are essential for effective communication. They represent the various purposes or intentions behind using language. By teaching language functions, students learn how to convey their thoughts, ideas, needs, and emotions accurately and appropriately in different contexts.

- **Real-Life Application**: Language functions are directly related to real-life situations. When students understand and can use language functions, they are better equipped to navigate everyday scenarios such as ordering food, asking for directions, making requests, and participating in conversations.

- **Cultural Awareness**: Language functions often carry cultural nuances and expectations. Teaching these functions helps students understand the cultural context of communication, promoting cultural awareness and sensitivity. This is particularly important in today's globalized world where people from diverse backgrounds interact regularly.

- **Pragmatic Competence**: Pragmatic competence refers to the ability to use language effectively in social and communicative situations. Teaching language functions enhances students' pragmatic competence by teaching them how to use language appropriately, including the use of politeness strategies, tone, and register.

- **Functional Fluency**: Language functions help students develop functional fluency. Instead of rote memorization of vocabulary and grammar rules, they learn how to apply language in meaningful ways. This leads to more confident and proficient language users.

- **Adaptability**: Language functions teach students how to adapt their language to different situations and interlocutors. This adaptability is crucial in both academic and professional settings where communication requirements vary.

- **Task-Based Learning**: Language functions provide a basis for task-based language learning. Educators can design activities and tasks that require students to use specific language functions, making the learning process more engaging and practical.

- **Interdisciplinary Skills**: Language functions can be integrated into various subjects and fields. By teaching language functions, students can apply their language skills to other disciplines, such as science, business, or healthcare, enhancing their overall academic and career readiness.

- **Improved Social Skills**: Language functions help students develop essential social skills such as active listening, empathy, and conflict resolution. These skills are valuable not only for language learners but also for personal and professional development.

- **Enhanced Critical Thinking**: Teaching language functions encourages critical thinking as students must analyze a situation and choose the most appropriate way to express themselves. This promotes cognitive development and problem-solving skills.

In summary, teaching English Language Functions is important because it equips learners with the practical communication skills they need to navigate a diverse and interconnected world. It goes beyond vocabulary and grammar, focusing on the functions of language in real-life contexts, ultimately leading to more effective and meaningful communication.

Lesson Plan: Teaching English Functions - Giving Directions

Level: Intermediate

Duration: 60 minutes

Objective: By the end of this lesson, students will be able to give and follow directions in English.

Materials: Map of a fictional town, whiteboard, markers, handouts, projector.

Engage (15 minutes):

1. **Warm-up Activity (5 minutes):** Start with a simple icebreaker to engage students. Ask each student to describe how they typically get to school or work. This will activate prior knowledge and introduce the topic of directions.
2. **Lead-In (10 minutes):** Show a map of a fictional town on the projector or whiteboard. Point to different locations on the

map (e.g., park, library, school, grocery store) and ask students questions like:
- "How would you go from the park to the library?"
- "Can you find the post office on the map?"
- "What's the quickest way to get from the school to the grocery store?"

Study (20 minutes):

1. **Vocabulary (5 minutes):** Introduce essential vocabulary related to giving directions such as "turn left," "turn right," "go straight," "take the first/second street on the left/right," "cross the road," and "opposite."
2. **Modeling (5 minutes):** Model giving directions by using the vocabulary and the map. For example: "To get from the park to the library, go straight down Main Street. Then, turn right onto Elm Street. The library is on your left."
3. **Practice (10 minutes):** Divide students into pairs. Provide each pair with a different set of directions between two locations on the map. Students take turns giving and following directions using the map and vocabulary. Encourage them to ask for clarification if needed.

Activation (20 minutes):

1. **Group Activity (10 minutes):** Have students work in small groups (3-4 students per group). Give each group a different starting point and a destination on the map. Each group must create and practice giving directions to reach the destination. They can use the vocabulary and phrases introduced earlier. After a few minutes, have each group present their directions to the class, either by acting them out or explaining them verbally.

2. **Role Play (10 minutes):** Organize a role-play activity. In pairs, one student plays the role of a lost tourist, and the other plays the role of a local giving directions. The tourist must ask for directions, and the local must provide clear and accurate instructions using the vocabulary learned. Rotate roles after a few minutes.

Closure (5 minutes):

1. **Discussion (3 minutes):** Ask students questions related to the lesson, such as:
    - "What was challenging about giving or following directions in English?"
    - "Why is it important to be able to give directions accurately?"
    - "Have you ever been in a situation where you needed to ask for directions in a foreign language?"
2. **Homework (2 minutes):** Assign homework, such as writing a short paragraph describing how to get from their home to a nearby landmark using the vocabulary and phrases learned in class.

Assessment: Observe students' participation in activities, their ability to give and follow directions accurately, and their use of vocabulary. Evaluate their homework for comprehension and application of the lesson.

Adaptations: Provide additional support for struggling students and challenge more advanced students with more complex directions or unfamiliar locations on the map.

Chapter 6

Teaching Skills and Techniques

6-1

Teaching Listening

Listening is a fundamental skill in language acquisition, and teaching listening in English is a critical component of English language education. Proficient listening skills enable learners to comprehend spoken language, engage in effective communication, and navigate various real-life situations. In this comprehensive article, we will delve into the importance of teaching listening, the challenges involved, effective strategies, and best practices to enhance listening skills in English language learners.

The Importance of Teaching Listening

1. Real-life Application: Listening is an essential skill for daily life, whether it be in conversations, meetings, or understanding media. Teaching listening equips learners with the ability to engage in meaningful interactions and interpret spoken information effectively.
2. Comprehension and Retention: Proficient listening skills are closely tied to comprehension and retention of information. When students can grasp what they hear, they are better prepared for academic success and professional opportunities.
3. Communication Proficiency: Effective listening is integral to effective communication. Teaching listening helps learners become

active and empathetic listeners, allowing them to respond appropriately in various social and professional contexts.

Challenges in Teaching Listening

Before diving into strategies, it is essential to acknowledge the challenges instructors and learners may encounter in teaching and learning listening skills in English:

1. Variability in Accents and Dialects: English is spoken with diverse accents and regional variations worldwide. Learners may struggle to understand speakers with different accents, which can hinder their listening comprehension.
2. Rate of Speech: Native speakers often speak quickly, which can pose challenges for learners. Understanding rapid speech requires well-honed listening skills.
3. Limited Exposure: Some English learners may not have regular exposure to native speakers or authentic listening materials, making it challenging to develop listening proficiency.
4. Lack of Visual Cues: Unlike reading or writing, listening does not provide visual cues. Learners must rely solely on their auditory skills, which can be intimidating for some.

Effective Strategies for Teaching Listening

1. Pre-listening Activities: a. Pre-teach Vocabulary: Introduce and explain key vocabulary and expressions that students will encounter in the listening task. b. Activate Background Knowledge: Discuss the topic or context of the listening activity to activate students' prior knowledge and build their anticipation.
2. During-listening Activities: a. Listen Multiple Times: Play the audio material multiple times, allowing students to become familiar with the content. b. Varied Listening Tasks: Use a variety of listening tasks such as multiple-choice questions, fill-in-the-blanks,

and comprehension questions to keep students engaged. c. Note-taking: Encourage students to take notes while listening to help them identify main ideas and important details.
3. Post-listening Activities: a. Group Discussions: After listening, have students discuss what they heard in pairs or small groups. This promotes reflection and encourages peer learning. b. Reflective Questions: Ask open-ended questions to help students analyze the content, express opinions, and make connections to their own lives. c. Summarization: Have students summarize the main points or the entire content in their own words.
4. Authentic Materials: a. Real-world Listening: Use authentic materials such as podcasts, news broadcasts, interviews, and movies to expose students to natural speech patterns and accents. b. Variety of Accents: Incorporate listening materials featuring speakers with diverse accents to prepare students for real-life communication.
5. Technology and Multimedia: a. Online Resources: Utilize online platforms, language learning apps, and multimedia tools to access a wide range of listening materials. b. Interactive Activities: Engage students in interactive listening activities like online quizzes and audio-based games.

Best Practices in Teaching Listening

1. Gradual Progression: Start with simple and shorter listening activities and gradually increase complexity as students' skills improve.
2. Active Engagement: Encourage students to actively listen by focusing on keywords, tone, and context.
3. Regular Practice: Incorporate listening activities into the curriculum regularly to reinforce and enhance skills over time.
4. Feedback and Assessment: Provide constructive feedback on students' listening performance and use assessment tools like listening tests to measure progress.

5. Cultural Awareness: Promote cultural sensitivity and awareness by discussing cultural nuances in spoken language.
6. Individualized Learning: Recognize that learners may have different strengths and weaknesses in listening skills, and tailor instruction to meet their needs.

Teaching listening in English is a crucial aspect of language education that empowers learners to communicate effectively and engage with the global community. By understanding the challenges and implementing effective strategies and best practices, educators can help students develop strong listening skills that will serve them well in various personal, academic, and professional contexts. Encouraging regular practice and exposure to authentic materials is key to fostering proficiency in this vital language skill.

6-2

Teaching Speaking

Speaking is a fundamental skill in language acquisition, and teaching it effectively in English is a crucial part of language education. The ability to communicate verbally in English opens doors to social, academic, and professional opportunities, making it essential for both ESL (English as a Second Language) learners and native speakers. In this comprehensive article, we will explore various strategies and approaches to teach speaking in English.

The Importance of Teaching Speaking in English

Effective communication in English is essential in our increasingly globalized world. Whether for travel, business, education, or social interaction, proficiency in speaking English can be a valuable asset. Here are some reasons why teaching speaking in English is important:

1. **Communication Skills:** Speaking is the primary mode of communication in everyday life. Teaching this skill helps individuals express their thoughts, ideas, and emotions effectively.
2. **Professional Advancement:** English is often the international language of business, science, and technology. Proficiency in spoken English can enhance career opportunities.
3. **Cultural Exchange:** Learning to speak English allows individuals to engage with people from diverse cultural backgrounds, fostering cross-cultural understanding and empathy.

4. **Academic Success:** English is widely used in academic settings. Strong speaking skills are essential for presentations, debates, and classroom discussions.
5. **Travel and Tourism:** English is commonly spoken in tourist destinations worldwide. Proficiency in spoken English facilitates travel and exploration.

Effective Strategies for Teaching Speaking in English

Now, let's delve into effective strategies for teaching speaking in English:

1. **Create a Supportive Environment:**
    - Encourage a classroom atmosphere where students feel comfortable speaking without fear of judgment.
    - Use icebreakers and team-building activities to build rapport among students.
2. **Role-Play and Simulations:**
    - Incorporate role-play scenarios relevant to real-life situations, such as ordering food in a restaurant or making a phone call.
    - Simulations allow students to practice conversational skills in a controlled setting.
3. **Use Authentic Materials:**
    - Incorporate authentic materials like podcasts, news broadcasts, and dialogues from movies or TV shows to expose students to natural spoken English.
    - This helps students become familiar with various accents, colloquialisms, and real-life conversations.
4. **Structured Conversations:**
    - Provide structured conversation prompts or topics to guide discussions.
    - Gradually increase the complexity of topics as students' proficiency improves.
5. **Peer Interaction:**

- Encourage students to interact with their peers through pair work and group discussions.
- Peer feedback can be valuable in identifying areas for improvement.

6. **Vocabulary Building:**
   - Teach vocabulary and phrases related to common speaking situations.
   - Use flashcards, games, and exercises to reinforce vocabulary acquisition.

7. **Pronunciation Practice:**
   - Focus on correct pronunciation and intonation patterns.
   - Use tongue twisters, listening exercises, and pronunciation drills to improve clarity.

8. **Recording and Self-Assessment:**
   - Have students record themselves speaking on various topics.
   - Encourage self-assessment and reflection to identify areas for improvement.

9. **Feedback and Correction:**
   - Provide constructive feedback on pronunciation, grammar, and fluency.
   - Correct errors gently and encourage self-correction.

10. **Cultural Context:**
    - Introduce cultural aspects and etiquette related to English-speaking countries.
    - Understanding cultural nuances can enhance communication.

11. **Technology Integration:**
    - Utilize language learning apps, online platforms, and virtual reality tools to make speaking practice engaging and interactive.

12. **Real-World Exposure:**

- Encourage students to participate in English-speaking clubs, attend cultural events, or engage in language exchange programs to apply their skills in real-life situations.

Assessment and Evaluation

Assessing and evaluating students' speaking abilities is crucial to track progress and determine areas that need improvement. Consider using various assessment methods, including:

1. **Oral Interviews:** One-on-one or small group interviews where students respond to prompts or engage in spontaneous conversation.
2. **Speaking Tests:** Structured tests that evaluate specific speaking skills, such as pronunciation, fluency, and vocabulary use.
3. **Peer Evaluation:** Peer assessment can provide valuable insights into a student's speaking abilities and encourage self-awareness.
4. **Self-Assessment:** Encourage students to assess their own speaking skills, set goals, and reflect on their progress.
5. **Portfolios:** Maintain speaking portfolios that include recordings, written reflections, and samples of students' speaking performance over time.

Teaching speaking in English is a multifaceted process that involves creating a supportive learning environment, incorporating a variety of teaching strategies, and continually assessing and providing feedback to students. Effective speaking skills open doors to personal and professional opportunities and empower individuals to connect with a global audience. By implementing the strategies outlined in this article and adapting them to the specific needs of your students, you can help them develop strong speaking abilities in English, enabling them to thrive in an increasingly interconnected world.

Teaching Reading

Reading is a fundamental skill in any language, and teaching reading in English is of paramount importance in today's globalized world. Proficiency in English reading not only opens up a world of knowledge and opportunities but also facilitates effective communication and critical thinking. In this comprehensive guide, we will delve into various aspects of teaching reading in English, including its importance, strategies, methods, and resources.

The Importance of Teaching Reading in English

1. Global Communication: English is one of the most widely spoken languages globally, serving as a lingua franca in many fields, including business, science, and diplomacy. Teaching reading in English enables individuals to communicate effectively in international contexts.
2. Access to Information: The majority of information on the internet, including scholarly articles, news, and research papers, is in English. Proficient readers can access a wealth of knowledge and stay updated on global developments.
3. Academic Success: English proficiency is often a prerequisite for academic success. Teaching reading skills early equips students

with the tools needed to excel in English-medium schools and universities.
4. Career Opportunities: Many job opportunities require English proficiency, and reading skills are essential for tasks like understanding manuals, reports, and emails in the workplace.

Effective Strategies for Teaching Reading in English

1. Phonics Instruction: Phonics is a method that focuses on teaching the relationship between letters and sounds. Beginning with phonics can help students decode words and build a strong foundation for reading.
2. Vocabulary Development: A rich vocabulary is crucial for comprehension. Encourage students to read widely and employ strategies like using context clues, dictionaries, and word walls to expand their vocabulary.
3. Comprehension Strategies: Teach students strategies like summarization, questioning, visualizing, and making connections to help them understand and remember what they read.
4. Fluency Practice: Fluent readers read smoothly and with expression. Regular reading practice and activities like choral reading, partner reading, and reader's theater can improve fluency.
5. Reading Aloud: Reading aloud to students, even in upper grades, enhances their listening comprehension, exposes them to new vocabulary, and models fluent reading.

Methods for Teaching Reading in English

1. Whole Language Approach: This approach emphasizes reading in context and encourages students to use their language skills to guess unfamiliar words based on the context.
2. Balanced Literacy: Balanced literacy combines both phonics-based instruction and whole language strategies, aiming to provide a well-rounded reading education.

3. Guided Reading: Small-group guided reading sessions allow teachers to provide tailored instruction to students at their specific reading levels.
4. Literature Circles: In literature circles, students read a chosen book and then discuss it in small groups. This approach fosters critical thinking and discussion skills.
5. Reading Workshops: Reading workshops provide students with independent reading time, during which they can choose books that interest them and engage in activities related to their reading.

Resources for Teaching Reading in English

1. Books: Utilize a wide range of reading materials, including fiction, non-fiction, picture books, novels, and magazines, to cater to various interests and reading levels.
2. Online Resources: Websites like Reading Rockets, Scholastic, and ReadWriteThink offer lesson plans, printable materials, and interactive activities for teaching reading.
3. Libraries: Regular visits to the school or local library can expose students to a diverse collection of books and encourage a love for reading.
4. Reading Apps: Educational apps like Raz-Kids, Epic, and ABCmouse provide interactive reading experiences that can engage and motivate young readers.
5. Reading Assessments: Tools like DIBELS (Dynamic Indicators of Basic Early Literacy Skills) and Fountas & Pinnell reading assessments help educators track students' progress and adjust instruction accordingly.

Teaching reading in English is a multifaceted endeavor that requires careful planning, a deep understanding of language acquisition, and a commitment to nurturing a love for reading. By using effective strategies, adopting appropriate methods, and leveraging available resources, educators can empower their students with the invaluable skill of

English reading. As a result, students can not only succeed academically but also navigate a world where English proficiency is a valuable asset.

Teaching Writing

Teaching writing in English is a vital skill that empowers individuals to communicate effectively, express their thoughts and ideas, and navigate the complexities of modern life. Whether you're an English teacher, a parent, or a writing tutor, understanding the strategies and best practices for teaching writing can make a significant difference in the development of strong writers. This comprehensive article explores various aspects of teaching writing in English, from the importance of writing to effective teaching strategies and assessment methods.

The Importance of Writing

Writing is a fundamental skill that transcends academic boundaries. It is a cornerstone of communication in both professional and personal spheres, enabling individuals to express themselves clearly and persuasively. Here are some reasons why teaching writing in English is so crucial:

1. **Communication:** Writing is a primary mode of communication in the digital age, used in emails, text messages, social media, and more. Proficiency in written communication is essential for success in various fields.

2. **Academic Success:** Writing is integral to academic achievement, with students required to write essays, reports, research papers, and more. Proficient writing skills are crucial for excelling in school and higher education.
3. **Critical Thinking:** Writing encourages critical thinking and analysis. When students write, they must organize their thoughts, synthesize information, and construct coherent arguments.
4. **Career Advancement:** Strong writing skills enhance career prospects. Employers value employees who can compose clear, concise, and persuasive documents, such as reports, proposals, and memos.
5. **Creative Expression:** Writing allows individuals to express their creativity, imagination, and unique perspectives. It is a means of self-discovery and personal growth.

Teaching Strategies for Writing in English

Effective teaching strategies play a pivotal role in nurturing strong writers. Here are some key strategies to consider when teaching writing in English:

1. **Modeling:** Teachers should model proficient writing by providing examples of well-written texts. This helps students understand the structure, style, and conventions of different types of writing.
2. **Process-Based Approach:** Encourage students to follow a writing process that includes prewriting, drafting, revising, editing, and proofreading. Emphasize that writing is a dynamic, iterative process.
3. **Feedback and Revision:** Provide constructive feedback on students' writing and encourage them to revise their work. Revision is essential for improving writing skills.
4. **Genre Awareness:** Teach students about different types of writing genres, such as narratives, essays, research papers, and

persuasive speeches. Each genre has its unique characteristics and conventions.
5. **Grammar and Mechanics:** Address grammar and mechanics as essential components of writing. Incorporate grammar lessons and editing exercises to improve students' language proficiency.
6. **Peer Review:** Foster a collaborative learning environment by incorporating peer review sessions. Peer feedback allows students to see different perspectives and improve their critical thinking skills.
7. **Writing Prompts:** Use thought-provoking writing prompts to inspire creativity and engage students' imaginations. Encourage them to explore a wide range of topics and themes.
8. **Technology Integration:** Leverage technology tools and platforms for writing assignments, such as word processors, grammar checkers, and online writing communities.

Assessment Methods

Assessing students' writing skills is crucial to monitor progress and provide targeted feedback. Consider these assessment methods:

1. **Rubrics:** Develop clear and specific rubrics that outline the criteria for evaluating writing assignments. This provides transparency and consistency in grading.
2. **Portfolio Assessment:** Create portfolios that showcase students' writing progress over time. Portfolios may include drafts, revisions, and final pieces, demonstrating growth and development.
3. **Peer Assessment:** Incorporate peer assessment where students evaluate each other's work based on predetermined criteria. This encourages self-reflection and enhances critical thinking.
4. **Self-Assessment:** Encourage students to reflect on their own writing skills, identifying strengths and areas for improvement. Self-assessment promotes self-awareness and self-directed learning.

5. **Standardized Tests:** Utilize standardized writing assessments like SAT or TOEFL to evaluate students' proficiency in academic and professional writing.
6. **Teacher Conferences:** Schedule one-on-one conferences with students to discuss their writing and provide personalized feedback. This approach allows for a deeper understanding of individual needs.

Challenges in Teaching Writing
Teaching writing in English can be challenging due to various factors:

1. **Diverse Student Needs:** Students come with diverse backgrounds, skills, and needs. Differentiating instruction is essential to address these variations.
2. **Motivation:** Some students may lack motivation for writing, viewing it as a chore rather than a valuable skill. Teachers should strive to make writing engaging and relevant.
3. **Time Constraints:** Teachers often have limited time to devote to writing instruction, given the demands of curriculum and testing requirements.
4. **Grading Workload:** Grading writing assignments can be time-consuming, especially for teachers with large classes. Effective grading strategies can help manage this workload.

Teaching writing in English is a multifaceted endeavor that requires patience, dedication, and adaptability. It is also immensely rewarding, as it equips students with a vital skill that will benefit them throughout their lives. By employing effective teaching strategies, thoughtful assessment methods, and an understanding of the challenges involved, educators can inspire and nurture proficient writers who can confidently express themselves in English, contributing to their academic success and personal growth. Ultimately, the ability to write effectively is a gift that keeps on giving, opening doors to opportunities and enriching lives.

6-5

Error Correction

Error correction is a fundamental aspect of language teaching, particularly in an English language classroom. It plays a crucial role in helping students improve their language proficiency by identifying and rectifying mistakes. However, the process of error correction can be complex, as it involves striking a balance between providing constructive feedback and maintaining a positive and encouraging learning environment. This article delves into the various strategies, approaches, and best practices for error correction in the English language classroom.

The Importance of Error Correction

Error correction serves multiple purposes in the English language classroom:

1. Reinforces Learning: Correcting errors helps students recognize and understand their mistakes, leading to better retention and comprehension of the language.
2. Builds Confidence: When errors are corrected effectively, students feel more confident in their ability to communicate in English.
3. Fosters Accuracy: Regular error correction aids in the development of linguistic accuracy, which is crucial for effective communication.

4. Enhances Fluency: By addressing errors, students can refine their language skills and ultimately become more fluent speakers and writers.

Error Correction Strategies

1. Immediate vs. Delayed Correction:
    - Immediate Correction: In this approach, the teacher corrects errors as soon as they occur, interrupting the student's speech. While it can be effective for addressing specific errors, it may hinder fluency and confidence.
    - Delayed Correction: Delayed correction involves noting down errors during a student's speech and addressing them after the speaking activity. This approach minimizes interruptions, allowing for more fluent communication.
2. Self-correction:
    - Encourage students to self-correct by providing them with opportunities to recognize and rectify their own mistakes. This approach promotes independent learning and self-awareness.
3. Peer Correction:
    - Peer correction involves students correcting each other's errors. This approach not only provides an additional perspective but also encourages collaboration and engagement among students.
4. Error Logs:
    - Encourage students to maintain error logs where they record their mistakes. Review these logs periodically to track progress and identify recurring errors.
5. Selective Correction:
    - Focus on correcting errors that hinder comprehension or are essential for clear communication. Prioritize higher-impact errors over minor ones to avoid overwhelming students.

Error Correction Approaches

1. Explicit Correction:
    - In explicit correction, the teacher directly points out the error, provides the correct form, and explains the rule or concept behind it. This approach is suitable for grammar and vocabulary errors.
2. Implicit Correction:
    - Implicit correction involves providing hints or cues to guide students toward the correct form without explicitly stating the error. This approach encourages critical thinking and problem-solving skills.
3. Reformulation:
    - Instead of directly correcting errors, the teacher repeats the incorrect sentence with the correct form, emphasizing the correction subtly. This approach maintains the flow of conversation while highlighting the mistake.
4. Error Identification:
    - In this approach, the teacher identifies the type of error (e.g., verb tense, subject-verb agreement) without providing the correct answer. Students are then tasked with correcting the error themselves, promoting active engagement.

Best Practices for Error Correction

1. Maintain a Positive Environment:
    - Ensure that error correction is conducted in a supportive and encouraging manner to prevent students from feeling discouraged or embarrassed.
2. Prioritize Fluency and Communication:
    - During speaking activities, emphasize the importance of effective communication over error-free speech to foster confidence and fluency.
3. Balance Correction Types:

- Use a combination of explicit and implicit correction strategies, tailoring your approach to the specific needs and preferences of your students.

4. Set Realistic Goals:
    - Understand that perfection is not the goal. Encourage progress and celebrate small victories in error reduction.
5. Individualized Feedback:
    - Provide personalized feedback to each student, addressing their unique strengths and weaknesses.
6. Use Technology:
    - Incorporate technology such as grammar-checking tools or language learning apps to supplement error correction activities.
7. Error Analysis:
    - Encourage students to analyze their errors, exploring why they made certain mistakes and how to avoid them in the future.

Error correction is an indispensable aspect of English language instruction. Effective error correction strategies and approaches can help students develop accuracy, fluency, and confidence in their language skills. By striking a balance between constructive feedback and a positive learning environment, educators can guide their students on the path to becoming proficient English speakers and writers. Remember that the ultimate goal is not to eliminate all errors but to foster growth and improvement in language proficiency.

6-6

Techniques for Correcting Writing Assignments

Effective writing is a crucial skill that students must develop to succeed academically and professionally. In an English classroom, one of the key responsibilities of educators is to help students improve their writing abilities. Correcting students' writing is an essential aspect of this process, as it provides valuable feedback and guidance for their growth as writers. However, it is equally important to employ techniques that are constructive, motivational, and tailored to individual needs. In this article, we will explore various techniques for correcting students' writing in an English classroom.

1. **Understand the Purpose of Correction**
   Before delving into specific techniques, it is essential to understand the purpose of correcting students' writing. Correction should not merely focus on identifying and marking errors but should aim to:
   a. Improve Clarity and Coherence: Ensure that the students' ideas are presented logically and clearly.
   b. Develop Language Skills: Help students enhance their vocabulary, grammar, and syntax.

c. Encourage Self-Reflection: Promote a culture of self-improvement, where students learn from their mistakes.

2. **Prioritize Feedback Over Grading**
   While grading is an integral part of assessing student performance, it should not overshadow feedback. Provide constructive feedback on students' writing by highlighting both strengths and areas for improvement. This positive reinforcement encourages students to view writing as a learning process rather than a mere task.

3. **Error Identification**
   a. Color-Coding: Use different colors to mark different types of errors (e.g., red for grammar, blue for punctuation). This visual distinction makes it easier for students to identify patterns in their mistakes.
   b. Symbols and Abbreviations: Develop a set of symbols and abbreviations to mark common errors, saving time and simplifying the correction process.
   c. Error Tally: Keep a tally of specific recurring errors and provide focused instruction on those issues to help students address them systematically.

4. **Peer Review**
   Peer review is a valuable technique that promotes collaborative learning and allows students to assess and correct each other's work. Encourage students to provide constructive feedback based on clear guidelines, such as focusing on content, organization, and language usage.

5. **Rubrics and Checklists**
   Create rubrics or checklists that outline the criteria for evaluating writing assignments. These tools provide students with clear expectations and help streamline the correction process. Rubrics can cover aspects like organization, clarity, coherence, grammar, and vocabulary usage.

6. **Individual Conferences**
   Hold one-on-one conferences with students to discuss their writing assignments. This personalized approach allows you to address their specific needs and concerns. During these conferences, provide feedback, answer questions, and offer guidance for improvement.

7. **Error Analysis**
   Encourage students to analyze their own writing for errors. Provide them with sample sentences or paragraphs containing errors, and ask them to identify and correct these errors independently. This self-assessment helps build critical thinking and problem-solving skills.

8. **Revision and Rewriting**
   Emphasize the importance of revision and rewriting. Encourage students to view their first draft as a rough sketch and subsequent drafts as opportunities for improvement. Offer feedback on multiple drafts to track their progress.

9. **Model Correct Writing**
   Provide model texts that showcase exemplary writing in terms of grammar, style, and structure. Analyze these texts with the class,

highlighting effective techniques and strategies that students can incorporate into their writing.

10. **Error Journals**

    Have students maintain error journals where they record recurring mistakes along with the correct versions. This practice encourages self-awareness and provides a handy reference for students to track their progress.

11. **Technology Tools**

Leverage technology tools such as grammar and spell-check software, online writing platforms, and plagiarism detectors to aid in the correction process. However, use them judiciously and ensure that students still engage in critical thinking and self-correction.

Correcting students' writing in an English classroom is a multifaceted process that requires a balanced approach. While addressing errors is crucial, it is equally important to foster a positive learning environment that encourages growth and self-improvement. By employing these techniques, educators can help students develop their writing skills, ultimately preparing them for success in their academic and professional endeavors. Remember that the goal is not just to correct, but to empower students to become more effective and confident writers.

Chapter 7

Linguistics for TESOL

7-1

Morphology

Morphology, a fundamental branch of linguistics, plays a crucial role in language acquisition and comprehension. In the context of an English language classroom, understanding morphology is essential for both teachers and students. Morphology deals with the structure and formation of words, encompassing elements such as prefixes, suffixes, roots, and affixes. This comprehensive article explores the significance of morphology in an English language classroom, its role in vocabulary acquisition, grammatical proficiency, and overall language proficiency enhancement.

I. Understanding Morphology

Before delving into the classroom implications, it's essential to grasp the basics of morphology. Morphology is concerned with the smallest meaningful units in a language, known as morphemes. A morpheme is the smallest grammatical unit that carries meaning, and it can be a word or part of a word. Morphemes are categorized into two main types: free morphemes, which can stand alone as words (e.g., "book," "run"), and bound morphemes, which must be attached to free morphemes to convey meaning (e.g., "-ed" in "walked," "-un" in "undo").

II. The Importance of Morphology in Vocabulary Acquisition

1. Word Formation Morphology is essential for understanding how words are created in English. By breaking down words into their constituent morphemes, students can deduce meanings of unfamiliar words. For instance, knowing that "unhappiness" is composed of "un-" (meaning not) and "happy" allows students to infer that it means not happy or sad.
2. Vocabulary Expansion Morphological awareness helps students expand their vocabulary. Learning common prefixes (e.g., "un-," "re-," "dis-") and suffixes (e.g., "-tion," "-able," "-ly") enables students to recognize and comprehend a wide range of words, even if they have never encountered them before. This facilitates effective reading and listening comprehension.

III. Enhancing Grammatical Proficiency

1. Verb Conjugation Morphology plays a crucial role in verb conjugation. English verbs often change form to indicate tense, aspect, or mood. For instance, the addition of "-ed" signifies past tense (e.g., "walked"), while "-ing" indicates present continuous tense (e.g., "walking"). Understanding these affixes is essential for students to construct grammatically correct sentences.
2. Noun and Adjective Formation Morphology also contributes to noun and adjective formation. Students can learn how to create nouns from verbs (e.g., "teach" becomes "teacher") and adjectives from nouns (e.g., "friend" becomes "friendly"). This knowledge enhances their ability to describe and classify objects and concepts in English.

IV. Morphology and Spelling

Morphological awareness is closely linked to spelling proficiency. Students who understand the morphological structure of words are better equipped to spell them correctly. For instance, knowing that "dis-" is a common prefix can help a student spell words like "disappear," "distrust," or "disagree" with ease.

V. Challenges and Teaching Strategies

1. Complex Morphology English morphology can be complex and inconsistent, leading to challenges for learners. Irregular verbs, for instance, do not follow typical conjugation patterns, making them harder to learn. Teachers must employ strategies such as mnemonics and practice exercises to help students master these irregularities.
2. Explicit Instruction Explicit instruction in morphology is crucial. Teachers can introduce students to common affixes, word families, and morphological rules. Interactive activities like word building games, puzzles, and word sorts can make the learning process engaging and effective.
3. Contextual Learning Morphology should be taught in context. Encouraging students to analyze the structure of words within sentences and texts helps them see the practical application of morphology in real communication.

In conclusion, morphology is a cornerstone of language learning and comprehension in an English language classroom. It not only aids vocabulary acquisition and grammatical proficiency but also contributes to improved spelling and reading skills. Teachers and students alike should recognize the significance of morphology as a foundational element of English language learning. By incorporating morphological instruction and exercises, educators can empower their students to become more proficient and confident English speakers, readers, and writers.

7-2

Syntax

Syntax is a fundamental aspect of language that governs how words are structured and organized to convey meaning. In an English language classroom, understanding and teaching syntax is essential for effective communication and language proficiency. This comprehensive guide explores the importance of syntax in language learning, its key components, and practical strategies for teaching and learning syntax in an English language classroom.

Understanding Syntax

Syntax refers to the set of rules and principles that govern sentence structure in a language. It encompasses the arrangement of words, phrases, and clauses to create well-formed and meaningful sentences. Syntax plays a pivotal role in conveying meaning, as it determines how words relate to one another within a sentence.

Key Components of Syntax

1. Word Order: Word order is a crucial element of syntax in English. English follows a subject-verb-object (SVO) word order in declarative sentences, such as "She (subject) loves (verb) ice cream (object)." Understanding word order is fundamental for constructing grammatically correct sentences.

2. Phrases and Clauses: Sentences are composed of smaller units known as phrases and clauses. A phrase is a group of words that functions as a single unit within a sentence, like "in the park." Clauses are larger units that contain a subject and a verb and can function independently as a sentence (independent clauses) or depend on another clause (dependent clauses).
3. Grammatical Roles: Each word in a sentence has a specific grammatical role, such as subject, verb, object, complement, or modifier. Understanding these roles helps learners create well-structured sentences.
4. Sentence Types: English sentences can be categorized into four main types: declarative (statements), interrogative (questions), imperative (commands), and exclamatory (expressions of strong emotion). Syntax determines the structure of each sentence type.

Importance of Syntax in Language Learning

1. Clarity and Communication: Proper syntax ensures that sentences are structured logically, making it easier for speakers and writers to convey their thoughts and ideas clearly. Inaccurate syntax can lead to misunderstandings and confusion.
2. Academic Success: Proficiency in syntax is crucial for academic success, as it enables students to write coherently and persuasively. Essays, research papers, and reports require well-structured sentences to effectively convey arguments and ideas.
3. Language Proficiency: Syntax is one of the key components evaluated in language proficiency tests like the TOEFL and IELTS. A strong grasp of syntax can significantly boost test scores.
4. Creative Expression: Understanding syntax allows learners to experiment with language and engage in creative writing, poetry, and storytelling.

Teaching Syntax in an English Language Classroom

1. Explicit Instruction: Teachers should provide explicit instruction on English syntax, including word order, sentence structure, and common grammatical rules. This can be done through lectures, worksheets, and exercises.
2. Sentence Diagramming: Sentence diagramming is a visual method that helps students analyze the structure of sentences. It involves breaking down sentences into their constituent parts and representing them graphically. This technique enhances students' understanding of syntax.
3. Error Correction: Regularly correcting syntax errors in students' writing and speech is essential for improvement. Provide constructive feedback and encourage students to revise and resubmit their work.
4. Syntax Games and Activities: Engaging and interactive activities, such as sentence-building games, word order competitions, and group discussions, can make learning syntax enjoyable and memorable.
5. Reading and Analysis: Encourage students to read a variety of texts, from literature to news articles, to expose them to different sentence structures. Analyzing these texts can help students understand how syntax is used in context.
6. Practice and Repetition: Syntax, like any other language skill, requires practice. Assign regular exercises and homework that focus on specific aspects of syntax, such as using different sentence types or rearranging words to form questions.

Challenges and Strategies for Learners

1. L1 Interference: Students whose native languages have different syntax patterns may struggle with English syntax. Recognizing and addressing these differences is important.
2. Complex Structures: English contains complex sentence structures, such as passive voice, relative clauses, and conditional

sentences. Break these down into manageable parts and provide step-by-step explanations.
3. Vocabulary and Collocation: Understanding word combinations (collocations) and the appropriate use of vocabulary within sentences is closely related to syntax. Encourage students to build their vocabulary and learn how words work together.

Syntax is a fundamental aspect of language learning in an English language classroom. It shapes how sentences are constructed, facilitating effective communication and academic success. By providing explicit instruction, engaging activities, and opportunities for practice, teachers can help students develop a strong grasp of English syntax, enabling them to express themselves more clearly and proficiently in both spoken and written language. Mastering syntax is a crucial step towards achieving fluency in English and becoming confident and effective communicators.

7-3 Semantics

Semantics is a fascinating and integral aspect of language learning, particularly in an English language classroom. It plays a pivotal role in helping learners comprehend the meaning of words, sentences, and texts, thereby enabling effective communication. Understanding semantics is not only essential for language acquisition but also for cultural and social integration. In this comprehensive article, we will delve into the world of semantics in an English language classroom, exploring its significance, key concepts, teaching strategies, and practical applications.

What is Semantics?
Semantics is the branch of linguistics that focuses on the study of meaning in language. It deals with how words, phrases, and sentences convey meaning and how people interpret and understand language. In the context of an English language classroom, semantics is about helping students grasp the meanings of English words, phrases, and sentences, as well as how they relate to each other.

Significance of Semantics in Language Learning

1. Vocabulary Acquisition: Semantics is fundamental to expanding one's vocabulary. Students must not only learn words but also

understand their meanings and how they are used in different contexts. A strong vocabulary is essential for effective communication and comprehension.
2. Reading Comprehension: Reading is a cornerstone skill in language learning. Semantics aids students in understanding the meaning of texts by deciphering word meanings, identifying synonyms and antonyms, and recognizing figurative language like metaphors and idioms.
3. Listening and Speaking: In spoken communication, semantics helps learners interpret the meaning behind spoken words and respond appropriately. It allows students to convey their ideas clearly and understand others effectively.
4. Writing Skills: Writing, too, relies heavily on semantics. Students need to select the right words and phrases to convey their intended message accurately. Additionally, understanding semantic relationships helps in constructing coherent and well-structured sentences and paragraphs.

Key Concepts in Semantics

1. Word Meaning: Word meaning can be categorized into two main types: denotation and connotation. Denotation refers to the literal, dictionary definition of a word, while connotation encompasses the emotional or cultural associations and nuances attached to a word.
2. Synonymy and Antonymy: Understanding synonyms (words with similar meanings) and antonyms (words with opposite meanings) is crucial for building a rich vocabulary and improving language comprehension.
3. Ambiguity: Semantics also deals with linguistic ambiguity, where a word, phrase, or sentence can have multiple interpretations. It's essential for learners to recognize and resolve ambiguity in language.

4. Polysemy: Polysemy refers to words that have multiple related meanings. For instance, the word "bank" can mean a financial institution or the side of a river. Teaching students to identify and use polysemous words correctly enhances their language proficiency.
5. Semantic Roles: In sentence structure, different words play specific semantic roles, such as the subject, object, or verb. Understanding these roles is crucial for constructing grammatically correct sentences.

Teaching Strategies for Semantics in the English Language Classroom

1. Contextual Learning: Encourage students to learn vocabulary in context rather than memorizing isolated words. Reading passages, authentic materials, and real-life situations help students grasp word meanings more effectively.
2. Word Mapping: Use semantic mapping techniques like word webs or semantic grids to visually represent the relationships between words and their meanings. This helps students understand connections and associations among words.
3. Vocabulary Games: Engaging vocabulary games, such as crossword puzzles, word searches, and semantic word associations, make learning fun and interactive. They also reinforce word meanings and usage.
4. Use of Visual Aids: Incorporate visual aids, such as images, videos, and illustrations, to reinforce word meanings. Visual stimuli can enhance students' understanding and retention of vocabulary.
5. Idiom and Metaphor Exploration: Teach idiomatic expressions and metaphors to enhance students' figurative language skills. Discuss the literal and figurative meanings of idioms to improve comprehension.
6. Encourage Discussion: Create opportunities for students to engage in discussions and debates, allowing them to apply their

understanding of semantics in real conversations. This fosters critical thinking and language production.

Practical Applications of Semantics in Language Learning

1. Exam Preparation: Semantics plays a crucial role in standardized tests like TOEFL, IELTS, and SAT. A solid understanding of word meanings and context helps students excel in these exams.
2. Literature Analysis: In literature classes, semantics aids in the analysis of literary works. Students can delve into the deeper meanings of texts, exploring themes, symbolism, and authorial intent.
3. Business and Professional Communication: Effective communication is vital in the workplace. A strong grasp of semantics helps professionals convey messages accurately and negotiate successfully.
4. Cross-Cultural Communication: Semantics is essential in understanding cultural nuances and avoiding misunderstandings in cross-cultural interactions. It promotes cultural sensitivity and adaptability.
5. Creative Writing: Writers use semantics to choose the right words and create vivid imagery in their writing. Understanding the nuances of language allows for more creative and impactful storytelling.

Semantics is the gateway to unlocking the power of meaning in an English language classroom. By emphasizing vocabulary acquisition, comprehension, and effective communication, semantics plays a pivotal role in language learning. Educators should integrate semantics into their teaching strategies, making language acquisition an engaging and enriching experience. Whether preparing for exams, analyzing literature, or navigating the professional world, a strong foundation in semantics equips students with the tools they need to succeed in their English language journey. Ultimately, semantics is not just about words; it's about connecting with others and expressing ideas in a meaningful way, fostering a global community of effective communicators.

7-4

Pragmatics

In an increasingly interconnected world, the importance of effective communication cannot be overstated. English has emerged as the lingua franca of global communication, and for non-native speakers, mastering not only the grammatical and lexical aspects but also the pragmatic dimension of the language is crucial. Pragmatics, the study of how language is used in context, plays a pivotal role in understanding and producing effective communication. In this article, we will explore the significance of pragmatics in an English language classroom, its impact on language acquisition, and practical strategies for teaching and learning pragmatic competence.

Understanding Pragmatics

Pragmatics is the branch of linguistics that investigates the ways in which language users convey meaning beyond the literal interpretation of words and sentences. It encompasses the study of speech acts, implicature, presupposition, and conversational implicature, among other aspects. In essence, pragmatics deals with the "how" of communication, focusing on the subtle nuances, social conventions, and context-dependent rules that govern language use.

Significance in Language Acquisition

1. Bridging Cultural Gaps: One of the foremost reasons for the significance of pragmatics in an English language classroom is its role in bridging cultural gaps. Different cultures have distinct norms and conventions regarding communication. Teaching pragmatics helps learners navigate these cultural differences and avoid misunderstandings. For example, the concept of politeness may vary greatly from one culture to another, and learners need to grasp these variations to communicate effectively.
2. Enhancing Communicative Competence: Communicative competence, as defined by linguist Dell Hymes, includes not only linguistic competence (grammar and vocabulary) but also sociolinguistic and pragmatic competence. Without a strong grasp of pragmatics, learners may have a limited ability to engage in real-world conversations. They may struggle to comprehend indirect speech acts, humor, sarcasm, and other non-literal language.
3. Pragmatic Transfer: Learners often transfer pragmatic norms from their native language into their English communication. This can lead to pragmatic errors, misinterpretations, or inappropriate language use. Explicit teaching of pragmatics can help learners identify such instances of pragmatic transfer and adapt their communication style to the target language.

Teaching Pragmatics in the English Language Classroom

Effective teaching of pragmatics requires a systematic and learner-centered approach. Here are some strategies for incorporating pragmatics into the English language classroom:

1. Explicit Instruction: Introduce key pragmatic concepts such as speech acts (e.g., requests, apologies, offers), politeness strategies, and indirect communication. Provide clear explanations and examples to help learners understand the principles of pragmatics.
2. Role-Play and Simulation: Engage learners in role-play activities that mimic real-life communicative situations. This allows them to practice using pragmatic strategies in context. For example,

learners can role-play job interviews, customer service interactions, or social gatherings.
3. Authentic Materials: Incorporate authentic materials like videos, podcasts, and texts that showcase natural language use. Analyze these materials with learners to highlight pragmatic elements such as tone, implied meanings, and conversational implicatures.
4. Cross-Cultural Awareness: Raise learners' awareness of cross-cultural differences in pragmatics. Encourage them to explore how politeness, politeness markers, and indirectness vary across cultures. This fosters cultural sensitivity and effective cross-cultural communication.
5. Error Correction and Feedback: Correct pragmatic errors gently and provide feedback on learners' use of pragmatics in real-world contexts. Encourage self-assessment and reflection on their communication experiences.
6. Contextualized Learning: Teach pragmatics in context, taking into account the learners' proficiency levels and communicative needs. Contextualized learning ensures that learners acquire pragmatic skills that are immediately applicable to their real-life situations.

Pragmatics is an integral part of language acquisition and effective communication in the English language classroom. By understanding and teaching pragmatics, educators can empower learners to navigate the complex web of social conventions, cultural norms, and context-dependent language use. The significance of pragmatics in an English language classroom lies not only in enhancing linguistic competence but also in fostering intercultural communication skills that are essential in our globalized world. Therefore, integrating pragmatics into language education is not just an option; it is a necessity for preparing learners to be proficient and culturally aware communicators in English.

Teaching Pronunciation and Phonology

Pronunciation and phonology play a pivotal role in language learning and communication. Effective pronunciation helps learners not only understand and be understood by others but also enhances their overall language proficiency. Teaching pronunciation and phonology is a crucial aspect of language instruction, as it enables learners to acquire the correct sounds, stress patterns, and intonation necessary for clear and effective communication. In this comprehensive guide, we will explore the importance of teaching pronunciation and phonology, discuss key concepts, methods, and strategies, and provide practical tips for educators and learners alike.

I. The Significance of Pronunciation and Phonology

1.1. Clear Communication Pronunciation and phonology are essential for clear communication in any language. Accurate pronunciation ensures that the intended message is conveyed effectively, reducing the chances of misunderstandings and miscommunication.

1.2. Social and Cultural Integration Correct pronunciation also plays a crucial role in the social and cultural integration of language learners. It allows them to feel more confident in their interactions with native speakers and helps them assimilate into their target language's cultural context.

1.3. Academic and Professional Success In academic and professional contexts, good pronunciation can significantly impact success. Language learners with strong pronunciation skills are better equipped to excel in oral exams, presentations, job interviews, and communication in the workplace.

II. Understanding Phonology

2.1. Phonemes Phonology deals with the study of phonemes, which are the smallest units of sound in a language. Understanding phonemes is essential for learners to differentiate between and produce the correct sounds in a language.

2.2. Minimal Pairs Minimal pairs are pairs of words that differ by only one phoneme, highlighting the significance of individual sounds in distinguishing word meanings. Teaching minimal pairs can help learners grasp the nuances of pronunciation.

2.3. Stress and Intonation Stress and intonation patterns are crucial elements of phonology. Stress refers to the emphasis placed on certain syllables within words, while intonation involves the rise and fall of pitch in speech. Both contribute to the natural rhythm and melody of spoken language.

III. Teaching Pronunciation and Phonology

3.1. Awareness and Exposure Creating awareness of phonological patterns and providing exposure to authentic pronunciation are fundamental. Language learners should listen to native speakers regularly to internalize correct pronunciation and intonation.

3.2. Visual and Auditory Aids Utilizing visual aids, such as phonetic charts, and auditory aids, like audio recordings or speech recognition software, can be highly effective in teaching pronunciation. These tools help learners associate written symbols with corresponding sounds.

3.3. Articulatory Feedback Incorporating techniques that focus on the physical aspects of pronunciation, such as tongue placement and lip movement, can be beneficial. Mirror exercises and hands-on guidance can help learners refine their articulation.

3.4. Corrective Feedback Providing constructive feedback is crucial. Corrective feedback should be specific, focusing on particular sounds or patterns that require improvement. Teachers should be encouraging and patient to motivate learners.

IV. Practical Strategies for Teaching Pronunciation

4.1. Pronunciation Drills Regular pronunciation drills can help learners practice specific sounds, words, or intonation patterns. These drills can be incorporated into lessons as warm-up exercises or dedicated practice sessions.

4.2. Dialogues and Role-Play Engaging learners in dialogues and role-play activities allows them to apply their pronunciation skills in real-life situations. This interactive approach helps learners build confidence and fluency.

4.3. Pronunciation Games and Activities Incorporating games and interactive activities, such as tongue twisters, pronunciation bingo, or word stress puzzles, can make pronunciation practice enjoyable and engaging for learners of all ages.

4.4. Peer and Self-Assessment Encouraging peer assessment and self-assessment can empower learners to take an active role in improving their pronunciation. Recording and evaluating their own speech can be a valuable tool for self-improvement.

V. Challenges and Solutions

5.1. L1 Interference One common challenge in teaching pronunciation is the interference of the learner's native language (L1) sounds and patterns. Teachers should be aware of these potential conflicts and provide targeted guidance to address them.

5.2. Accent Variation Accepting accent variation is important in language instruction. While clarity is crucial, learners should not feel pressured to eliminate their accents entirely. Focus on intelligibility rather than accent reduction.

5.3. Teacher Training Effective pronunciation teaching requires educators to be well-trained in phonology. Professional development and ongoing training for teachers can enhance their ability to support learners in this area.

Teaching pronunciation and phonology is an essential component of language instruction, contributing to effective communication, cultural integration, and academic or professional success. By understanding the key concepts, methods, and strategies outlined in this comprehensive guide, educators can help learners master the intricacies of pronunciation and phonology. Empowering language learners with the skills and confidence to communicate clearly and effectively is a valuable gift that will serve them well throughout their lives.

7-6

Stress and Intonation

English, as a global lingua franca, has become an essential language to master for many people worldwide. Whether you're learning English for academic, professional, or personal reasons, one of the crucial aspects of mastering the language is understanding stress and intonation. These linguistic features play a significant role in conveying meaning and effective communication. In the realm of English Language Teaching (ELT), understanding stress and intonation is vital for both learners and educators. In this comprehensive article, we will delve into the importance of stress and intonation in English, their role in communication, teaching methods, and strategies to effectively teach and learn these essential elements.

Understanding Stress in English

Stress, in the context of linguistics, refers to the relative emphasis or prominence given to certain syllables or words within a sentence. Stress can drastically alter the meaning of a sentence, making it a critical element in English pronunciation and comprehension. In the English language, stress typically falls on syllables, not individual vowels or consonants. Stress patterns vary depending on the word and its grammatical role in a sentence. Here are some key aspects of stress in English:

1. Word Stress: English words typically have one syllable that is stressed more than the others. This is often the first syllable in nouns, adjectives, and adverbs but can vary in verbs. For example, in the word "photograph," the stress falls on the second syllable, so it is pronounced as "PHO-tuh-graf."
2. Sentence Stress: Stress isn't limited to individual words; it also applies to sentences. English speakers emphasize certain words or syllables to convey the intended meaning and emotion. Understanding sentence stress is crucial for effective communication.
3. Content Words vs. Function Words: Content words, such as nouns, verbs, adjectives, and adverbs, typically receive stress, while function words like articles, prepositions, and conjunctions are typically unstressed. For instance, in the sentence "She is reading a book," the content words "reading" and "book" receive stress.
4. Shifts in Stress: Stress can change based on whether a word is used as a noun or a verb. For example, the noun "record" is pronounced with stress on the first syllable ("RE-cord"), while the verb "record" is pronounced with stress on the second syllable ("re-CORD").

Understanding Intonation in English

Intonation refers to the rising and falling patterns of pitch in spoken language. It is used to convey various aspects of communication, including mood, attitude, and emphasis. While stress focuses on individual words or syllables, intonation shapes the entire sentence and, by extension, the conversation. Here are some key elements of intonation in English:

1. Pitch Patterns: English speakers use rising and falling pitch patterns to indicate questions, statements, and emotions. For instance, a rising pitch at the end of a sentence usually indicates a question, while a falling pitch suggests a statement.
2. Emotion and Attitude: Intonation also reflects the speaker's emotions and attitude. A speaker can sound enthusiastic, curious,

annoyed, or indifferent based on their intonation. This aspect of intonation can significantly impact effective communication.
3. Contrast and Emphasis: Intonation can highlight important information within a sentence. By raising the pitch on specific words or phrases, a speaker can emphasize their importance and guide the listener's understanding.

Importance of Stress and Intonation in English Language Teaching

In English Language Teaching, understanding stress and intonation is paramount for several reasons:

1. Effective Communication: Correct stress and intonation help learners convey their intended message clearly and accurately. Misplaced stress or incorrect intonation can lead to misunderstandings, even if the grammar and vocabulary are correct.
2. Natural Speech Patterns: Stress and intonation make spoken English sound natural. Learners who master these elements are more likely to be understood and perceived as fluent speakers.
3. Listening Comprehension: Proficiency in stress and intonation is crucial for comprehending spoken English, especially in real-life situations. Learners who understand the variations in pitch and stress are better equipped to understand native speakers.
4. Cultural Awareness: Intonation can also reveal cultural nuances and norms. Understanding the emotional and social aspects conveyed through intonation is vital for effective cross-cultural communication.

Teaching Stress and Intonation

Teaching stress and intonation in English can be a complex but rewarding endeavor. Effective teaching methods can help students grasp these elements of spoken language more easily. Here are some strategies for teaching stress and intonation:

1. Contextualization: Teach stress and intonation in the context of real-life conversations. Use authentic materials like audio recordings, podcasts, and videos to show how these elements work in practice.
2. Listen and Repeat: Encourage students to listen to native speakers and repeat sentences, focusing on mimicking stress and intonation patterns. This practice helps learners internalize these features.
3. Visual Aids: Visual representations of stress and intonation, such as stress marks or pitch contours, can be beneficial. These visual aids can help learners see and understand the patterns.
4. Interactive Activities: Engage students in interactive activities that require them to use stress and intonation actively. Role-plays, debates, and discussion exercises can be particularly useful.
5. Feedback and Practice: Provide constructive feedback on students' pronunciation, stress, and intonation. Encourage regular practice and self-assessment.

Learning Stress and Intonation

For English learners, mastering stress and intonation involves active engagement and practice. Here are some tips for effectively learning stress and intonation:

1. Listen Actively: Listen to a variety of English speakers, paying close attention to their stress and intonation patterns. Focus on different accents and dialects to develop a well-rounded understanding.
2. Record Yourself: Record your speech and compare it to native speakers. This self-assessment can help identify areas that need improvement.
3. Practice Regularly: Engage in speaking exercises that focus on stress and intonation. Repeat sentences, engage in role-plays, and participate in speaking clubs or online forums to practice with others.

4. Receive Feedback: Seek feedback from teachers, language partners, or online communities. Constructive criticism can help you make necessary adjustments to your pronunciation.
5. Explore Resources: Utilize online resources, such as pronunciation apps and websites that offer interactive exercises and practice materials for stress and intonation.

Stress and intonation are essential components of spoken English that significantly impact communication and comprehension. In the field of English Language Teaching, instructors play a pivotal role in helping learners understand and utilize stress and intonation effectively. Learners, in turn, need to engage actively in practice and self-assessment to master these elements of spoken language. With the right teaching methods and dedicated effort, learners can enhance their pronunciation, making them more confident and effective communicators in English, and thus furthering their goals in both personal and professional spheres.

Chapter 8

Lesson Planning

Lesson Planning

Lesson planning is a crucial aspect of effective teaching in any subject, but it holds particular significance in an English language classroom. English is a global language, and proficiency in it is essential for communication, academic success, and career advancement. Therefore, lesson planning in an English language classroom requires careful consideration of various factors to ensure that students acquire the necessary language skills and knowledge. In this comprehensive guide, we will explore the importance of lesson planning in an English language classroom, the key components of effective lesson plans, and some best practices for successful implementation.

The Importance of Lesson Planning

Lesson planning is often described as the roadmap that guides teachers and students through the learning process. In an English language classroom, effective lesson planning is of paramount importance for several reasons:

1. Meeting Curriculum Goals

Lesson plans help ensure that teachers cover all the essential topics and language skills outlined in the curriculum. This is crucial for achieving academic standards and ensuring that students are adequately prepared for assessments.

2. Maximizing Classroom Time

Well-structured lesson plans make the most of limited classroom time. They enable teachers to present content efficiently, engage students in meaningful activities, and provide opportunities for practice and reinforcement.

3. Addressing Diverse Learning Needs

In an English language classroom, students often come from diverse linguistic backgrounds and have varying levels of proficiency. Lesson plans should be designed to accommodate these differences, providing support and challenge as needed.

4. Fostering Engagement and Motivation

Engaging lesson plans with clear objectives and engaging activities can motivate students to actively participate in the learning process. When students are motivated, they are more likely to retain information and make progress.

5. Effective Assessment

Lesson plans should include assessment strategies that allow teachers to measure student progress accurately. This information helps educators make informed decisions about adjusting their teaching methods to meet individual and class-wide needs.

Key Components of Effective Lesson Plans

To create effective lesson plans in an English language classroom, teachers should include the following key components:

1. Clear Learning Objectives

Every lesson plan should begin with clear, specific learning objectives. These objectives define what students should know or be able to do by the end of the lesson. Objectives should be measurable and aligned with curriculum standards.

2. Pre-assessment

Before introducing new content, it is essential to assess what students already know about the topic. Pre-assessment helps teachers tailor instruction to meet the needs of their students and avoid unnecessary repetition.

3. Introduction

The introduction sets the stage for the lesson. It can include an engaging hook to capture students' attention, a brief overview of the lesson's objectives, and a connection to prior learning to provide context.

4. Main Content

The main content section of the lesson plan outlines the core information or language skills students will acquire. This can include vocabulary, grammar rules, reading passages, or speaking and listening activities. It's crucial to scaffold learning, starting with simple concepts and progressively building complexity.

5. Activities and Strategies

Lesson plans should incorporate a variety of engaging activities and instructional strategies. These can include group discussions, pair work, role-plays, debates, multimedia presentations, and hands-on activities. The choice of activities should align with the lesson's objectives and cater to different learning styles.

6. Assessment and Feedback

Incorporate formative assessment strategies throughout the lesson to gauge student understanding. Provide immediate feedback to help students identify their strengths and areas for improvement. Summative assessments at the end of the lesson can help measure overall comprehension.

7. Closure

A proper lesson closure summarizes the key points of the lesson, reviews the learning objectives, and provides an opportunity for students to reflect on what they have learned. It can also include a preview of the next lesson to create continuity in learning.

8. Materials and Resources

List all materials, resources, and technology needed for the lesson. This includes textbooks, worksheets, audiovisual aids, and digital tools. Ensuring that these resources are readily available is essential for smooth lesson delivery.

9. Adaptations and Differentiation

Consider how you will adapt the lesson for students with diverse learning needs, such as English language learners or students with learning disabilities. Differentiation strategies can include modified materials, additional support, or enriched activities for advanced learners.

Best Practices for Successful Lesson Planning

To enhance the effectiveness of lesson planning in an English language classroom, teachers can follow these best practices:

1. Know Your Students

Understanding your students' proficiency levels, interests, and individual needs is crucial for effective lesson planning. Differentiation and adaptation should be informed by this knowledge.

2. Align with Curriculum Standards

Ensure that your lesson plans align with the curriculum standards and learning objectives established by your educational institution or governing body.

3. Keep Learning Objectives Clear

Learning objectives should be written in language that is easy for students to understand and measurable so that you can assess whether they have been achieved.

4. Incorporate Real-Life Applications

Connect language learning to real-life situations and practical use. This makes the content more relevant and engaging for students.

5. Use Varied Assessment Methods

Incorporate a mix of assessment methods, including formative assessments during the lesson and summative assessments at the end. This provides a comprehensive view of student progress.

6. Provide Opportunities for Student Reflection

Encourage students to reflect on their learning experience. This can be done through journal writing, class discussions, or self-assessment activities.

7. Be Flexible

Be prepared to adapt your lesson plan based on the needs and interests of your students. Flexibility is key to effective teaching.

8. Seek Professional Development

Continuously improve your lesson planning skills through professional development opportunities, workshops, and collaboration with colleagues.

In conclusion, lesson planning in an English language classroom is a multifaceted process that requires careful consideration of various elements. Effective lesson plans are essential for meeting curriculum goals, engaging students, and fostering language proficiency. By following the key components and best practices outlined in this comprehensive guide, teachers can create well-structured and engaging lesson plans that support student learning and success in the English language.

Chapter 9

Course Materials

9-1

Effective Use of Materials in the Classroom

The use of materials in an English language classroom plays a pivotal role in creating an engaging and effective learning environment. Educational materials encompass a wide range of resources, including textbooks, multimedia, realia, props, and digital tools. Integrating these materials strategically into lessons can significantly enhance the teaching and learning experience. This article explores the importance of using materials in an English language classroom, offers insights into various types of materials, and provides practical tips for their effective utilization.

The Significance of Using Materials

1. Fostering Active Learning: Utilizing materials encourages active participation among students. Instead of passively absorbing information, learners engage with the material, which promotes critical thinking and problem-solving skills.
2. Enhancing Retention: Visual aids and tangible objects help students remember information better. The use of materials taps into multiple sensory modalities, making it easier for learners to retain what they have learned.

3. Catering to Diverse Learning Styles: Every student has a unique learning style, and materials can be tailored to accommodate these differences. Visual learners benefit from images and charts, kinesthetic learners thrive with hands-on activities, and auditory learners may prefer multimedia resources.
4. Increasing Motivation: Incorporating materials can make lessons more engaging and enjoyable for students. When lessons are interactive and interesting, students are more motivated to participate and learn.

Types of Materials in the English Language Classroom

1. Textbooks: Traditional textbooks remain a valuable resource in language education. They provide structured content, grammar explanations, and exercises to reinforce language skills. Teachers can supplement textbooks with additional materials for a well-rounded curriculum.
2. Multimedia: Videos, audio recordings, and interactive software can bring real-world language usage into the classroom. They expose students to various accents, colloquialisms, and cultural nuances, helping them develop listening and speaking skills.
3. Realia: Realia refers to authentic, everyday items from the target culture, such as newspapers, maps, menus, and clothing. Incorporating realia into lessons helps students connect language to real-life situations and cultural contexts.
4. Visual Aids: Visual aids, including charts, graphs, diagrams, and posters, assist in conveying complex information. These aids are particularly useful for explaining grammar rules, vocabulary, and conceptual ideas.
5. Props and Manipulatives: Physical objects like flashcards, puzzles, and models provide hands-on learning opportunities. They are excellent tools for teaching vocabulary, sentence structure, and concepts in a tactile manner.

6. Digital Resources: In today's technology-driven world, there is an abundance of digital resources available. These include language learning apps, websites, and software programs that offer interactive exercises, quizzes, and immersive language experiences.

Effective Use of Materials

1. Align with Learning Objectives: Select materials that align with your lesson objectives. Ensure that the materials support the language skills you want to develop, whether it's listening, speaking, reading, or writing.
2. Incorporate Variety: Use a mix of materials to keep lessons dynamic. For example, pair a textbook reading with a related video or follow a grammar exercise with a realia-based activity. Variety keeps students engaged and prevents monotony.
3. Adapt to Student Proficiency Levels: Tailor the complexity of materials to the proficiency levels of your students. Beginners may require simplified materials with more visuals, while advanced learners can handle more complex texts and resources.
4. Promote Interaction: Encourage students to interact with materials and with each other. Group activities, role-plays, and discussions based on materials create opportunities for authentic language use and communication.
5. Provide Context: Always provide context when introducing materials. Explain why a particular resource is relevant to the lesson and how it connects to real-life situations or cultural insights.
6. Evaluate and Update: Regularly assess the effectiveness of the materials you use. Solicit feedback from students and adjust your approach accordingly. Be open to replacing or updating materials as needed to meet evolving educational goals.

Incorporating materials into the English language classroom is an essential pedagogical strategy that enhances the learning experience for students. These materials provide opportunities for active learning, cater to diverse learning styles, and make lessons more engaging and memorable. By carefully selecting and effectively utilizing materials that align with learning objectives, teachers can create a dynamic and enriching classroom environment that promotes language acquisition and cultural understanding. Ultimately, the judicious use of materials empowers both teachers and students in their quest to master the English language.

Chapter 10

Assessment and Testing

10-1

Formative and Summative Assessments

Formative and summative assessments are two distinct types of assessments used in education to evaluate student learning and performance. They serve different purposes and are typically used at different stages of the learning process.

1. **Formative Assessment:**
    - Purpose: Formative assessment is used to gather information about students' learning progress during the instructional process. It helps teachers understand what students know, what they don't know, and where they might be struggling. The primary purpose is to provide feedback and guide instruction.
    - Timing: Formative assessments are conducted throughout the learning process, often on a daily or weekly basis. They are ongoing and are used to make adjustments to instruction as needed.
    - Examples: Classroom discussions, quizzes, homework assignments, group activities, peer assessments, self-assessments, and teacher observations.

- Feedback: Formative assessment feedback is usually immediate and specific, focusing on areas where students need improvement.

2. **Summative Assessment:**
    - Purpose: Summative assessment is used to evaluate and measure what students have learned at the end of a specific period or unit of instruction. It is used to assign grades, make judgments about student achievement, and determine whether learning objectives have been met.
    - Timing: Summative assessments are typically administered at the end of a grading period, semester, or school year. They are not intended to guide instruction but rather to provide a summary of what students have learned.
    - Examples: Final exams, standardized tests, end-of-term projects, research papers, and state assessments.
    - Feedback: Summative assessment feedback is often delayed, as it occurs after the completion of the learning period. It is typically focused on the overall performance of the student.

In summary, formative assessments are designed to inform instruction and help students learn and improve, while summative assessments are used to evaluate and measure the final outcomes of learning. Both types of assessments have their place in education, with formative assessments supporting the learning process and summative assessments providing a summary of a student's overall achievement. Effective educators often use a combination of both formative and summative assessments to gain a comprehensive understanding of student progress and learning outcomes.

Rubrics and Assessment

Rubrics and assessment criteria are tools used in education and various other fields to evaluate and assess the quality and performance of tasks, assignments, projects, or any other form of work. They provide clear guidelines and standards for assessing and scoring work consistently and objectively. Rubrics and assessment criteria are particularly useful for educators, instructors, employers, and evaluators to provide feedback and make informed judgments about the performance or quality of a task. Here's a breakdown of these terms:

1. **Rubrics:**
    - **Definition**: A rubric is a scoring guide or a set of criteria used to evaluate and assess a piece of work or performance. It consists of a matrix or table that outlines specific criteria, levels of achievement, and descriptors for each level.
    - **Purpose**: Rubrics help ensure consistency and fairness in the evaluation process by providing clear expectations and standards for what is being assessed.
    - **Components of a Rubric:**
        - **Criteria**: The specific elements or dimensions that are being assessed. These criteria should be well-defined and relevant to the task.

- **Levels of Achievement**: Different levels or categories that indicate the degree of performance or quality, typically ranging from low to high (e.g., "poor," "fair," "good," "excellent").
- **Descriptors**: Clear descriptions or explanations of what constitutes each level of achievement for each criterion.
- **Example**: A rubric for assessing a research paper might include criteria such as "Thesis Statement," "Organization," "Research Depth," and levels of achievement like "Limited," "Satisfactory," "Proficient," and "Exceptional."

2. **Assessment Criteria**:
   - **Definition**: Assessment criteria are the specific standards or benchmarks used to judge the quality or performance of a task or work. They can be a part of a rubric or used independently.
   - **Purpose**: Assessment criteria provide the basis for evaluating and making judgments about the quality of work. They help assessors determine whether the work meets predefined standards.
   - **Flexibility**: Assessment criteria can be tailored to the specific task or assessment. They allow for customization to fit the unique requirements of different assignments or projects.
   - **Example**: In a writing assignment, the assessment criteria might include factors like "Clarity of Writing," "Use of Evidence," "Grammar and Spelling," and "Overall Coherence."

The process of using rubrics and assessment criteria typically involves the following steps:

1. **Design**: Create a rubric or define assessment criteria that are relevant to the task or assignment being assessed.
2. **Communicate Expectations**: Share the rubric or criteria with the individuals being assessed, ensuring they understand what is expected.
3. **Assessment**: Evaluate the work based on the criteria and levels of achievement specified in the rubric or assessment criteria.
4. **Feedback**: Provide feedback to the individuals or students, referencing the rubric or criteria to explain areas of strength and areas for improvement.
5. **Scoring**: Assign scores or ratings based on the rubric or assessment criteria.
6. **Summative Evaluation**: Use the scores or assessments to make informed judgments about the overall quality or performance.

Rubrics and assessment criteria are valuable tools for promoting transparency, consistency, and fairness in assessment processes, whether in education, performance evaluations, or other contexts where evaluation and feedback are essential.

10-3

Feedback and Grading

Feedback and grading are essential components of teaching English, as they help students understand their progress, identify areas for improvement, and motivate them to continue learning. Here are some key principles and strategies for providing effective feedback and grading in teaching English:

1. **Clear Learning Objectives:**
    - Clearly communicate learning objectives and expectations to students at the beginning of each lesson or assignment. This helps them understand what is expected of them.

2. **Formative vs. Summative Assessment:**
    - Use both formative and summative assessments. Formative assessments are ongoing assessments used to provide feedback for learning, while summative assessments evaluate what students have learned.

3. **Timely Feedback:**
    - Provide feedback promptly, ideally as soon as possible after the assessment or assignment. Timely feedback helps students connect their efforts with the outcomes.

4. **Specific and Constructive Feedback:**
   ◦ Be specific in your feedback. Instead of simply saying, "Good job," provide detailed comments on what was done well and what could be improved. Use constructive language to suggest ways for improvement.

5. **Use of Rubrics:**
   ◦ Develop and share rubrics with students to outline grading criteria. Rubrics make your grading process more transparent and help students understand how they will be assessed.

6. **Peer Feedback:**
   ◦ Encourage peer feedback. This can be an effective way for students to learn from each other and gain different perspectives on their work.

7. **Individualized Feedback:**
   ◦ Recognize that every student is unique and may have different strengths and weaknesses. Tailor your feedback to address each student's specific needs.

8. **Positive Reinforcement:**
   ◦ Highlight students' strengths and achievements to boost their confidence and motivation. Positive reinforcement can inspire students to continue learning.

9. **Encourage Self-Assessment:**
    - Teach students to self-assess their work. This helps them take ownership of their learning and become more reflective learners.

10. **Goal Setting:**
    - Work with students to set specific, achievable goals based on their current abilities and areas for improvement. Regularly revisit these goals to track progress.

11. **Communication:**
    - Maintain open communication with students. Encourage them to ask questions and seek clarification on your feedback.

12. **Fair and Consistent Grading:**
    - Ensure fairness and consistency in grading by adhering to the established rubrics and criteria. Avoid grading bias and favoritism.

13. **Grade Reflective of Learning Outcomes:**
    - Ensure that the final grade reflects the student's understanding of the content and their progress in developing language skills.

14. **Feedback Formats:**
    - Use various formats for feedback, including written comments, verbal feedback, and digital tools (e.g., track changes in a document, audio comments).

15. **Cultural Sensitivity:**
    - Be aware of cultural differences in communication and assessment. Avoid making judgments based on cultural norms or stereotypes.

16. **Data Tracking:**
    - Keep records of student progress over time. This helps you identify patterns and make data-informed decisions about instructional adjustments.

17. **Growth Mindset:**
    - Encourage a growth mindset in students by emphasizing that mistakes are opportunities for learning and improvement.

18. **Feedback for Different Language Skills:**
    - Tailor feedback to address various language skills, such as listening, speaking, reading, and writing, depending on the context of the assessment.

Remember that effective feedback and grading are ongoing processes that should support students in their English language learning journey. Continuously assess and refine your feedback and grading methods to meet the evolving needs of your students.

Chapter 11

Specialized TESOL Contexts

ND# Teaching Business English

eaching Business English is a specialized field within the realm of English language teaching (ELT) that focuses on equipping students with the language skills and cultural knowledge necessary to excel in the world of business and commerce. As the global economy becomes increasingly interconnected, the demand for proficient English speakers in professional settings continues to grow. Therefore, the role of educators in preparing individuals to navigate the intricacies of the business world has never been more crucial.

In this comprehensive guide, we will delve into the key aspects of teaching Business English, including the importance of this specialized branch of language teaching, strategies for effective instruction, curriculum development, and assessment methods. Whether you are a seasoned educator looking to refine your skills or a novice teacher interested in exploring this field, this article will provide valuable insights and practical tips to help you succeed.

1. Understanding the Importance of Business English

1.1. Globalization and Communication

The rapid globalization of markets and businesses has made English the de facto international language of commerce. Professionals worldwide need to communicate effectively in English to engage in international trade, negotiations, and collaborations. Teaching Business English helps individuals bridge language barriers and seize global opportunities.

1.2. Career Advancement

Proficiency in Business English is often a key factor in career advancement. Many multinational companies prefer employees who can communicate confidently and fluently in English, as it enhances their ability to work with international clients, colleagues, and partners.

1.3. Cultural Competence

Business English also encompasses cultural awareness and understanding. In the global business arena, cultural nuances and etiquette play a significant role. Teaching Business English goes beyond grammar and vocabulary; it involves imparting cultural competence, which is essential for building successful cross-cultural relationships.

2. Strategies for Effective Instruction

2.1. Needs Analysis

Before embarking on teaching Business English, it's essential to conduct a thorough needs analysis. Understand your students' specific goals, backgrounds, industries, and language proficiency levels. This analysis will inform your teaching approach and help tailor your lessons to meet the learners' needs.

2.2. Business English Content

Business English curriculum often covers a wide range of topics, such as business communication, negotiations, presentations, and professional writing. Ensure that your lessons are relevant to the students' real-world needs, incorporating industry-specific terminology and scenarios.

2.3. Authentic Materials

Incorporating authentic materials, such as business reports, articles, emails, and videos, can make the learning experience more engaging and practical. These materials expose students to real-world language use and help them develop language skills that are directly applicable in their professional lives.

2.4. Role-Playing and Simulation

Role-playing and simulation exercises can be invaluable in teaching Business English. Create scenarios where students can practice business meetings, negotiations, and presentations. These activities allow learners to apply language skills in a controlled yet realistic environment.

2.5. Business Etiquette

Teaching Business English should also include lessons on business etiquette and cultural norms. Topics like appropriate greetings, dress codes, and communication styles can significantly impact a professional's success in a multicultural workplace.

3. Curriculum Development

3.1. Framework

Develop a comprehensive curriculum that outlines the scope and sequence of your Business English course. Consider structuring it around language skills (listening, speaking, reading, and writing), specific business topics, and cultural competencies.

3.2. Learning Objectives

Clearly define the learning objectives for each module or lesson. Learning objectives should be specific, measurable, achievable, relevant, and time-bound (SMART), ensuring that students and instructors have a clear understanding of what is expected.

3.3. Assessment

Design assessments that align with your learning objectives. Assessments can include written assignments, presentations, role-plays, or even mock business meetings. Regular feedback and assessment are critical for tracking student progress and adjusting your teaching strategies accordingly.

3.4. Flexibility

Be prepared to adapt your curriculum as needed. Business environments are dynamic, and language needs can change. Stay updated with industry trends and adjust your curriculum to reflect current business practices.

4. Assessment Methods

4.1. Formative Assessment

Formative assessments, conducted throughout the learning process, help instructors gauge student understanding and identify areas that need improvement. These can include quizzes, group discussions, and peer evaluations.

4.2. Summative Assessment

Summative assessments are typically conducted at the end of a course or module to evaluate overall learning outcomes. They can take the form of final exams, presentations, or projects. Ensure that these assessments align with the course objectives.

4.3. Portfolios

Encourage students to maintain portfolios of their work, which can include written assignments, presentations, and other project-based tasks. Portfolios provide a holistic view of a student's progress over time.

4.4. Self-Assessment

Foster a culture of self-assessment, where students reflect on their language proficiency and set personal learning goals. Encourage them to identify areas for improvement and take ownership of their language development.

Teaching Business English is a rewarding endeavor that equips individuals with the language and cultural competencies they need to thrive in the global business landscape. As educators, it is our responsibility to provide students with the knowledge and skills they require to communicate effectively, build successful careers, and contribute to the global economy.

By understanding the importance of Business English, implementing effective teaching strategies, developing a relevant curriculum, and employing various assessment methods, educators can prepare their students to excel in the competitive world of business. As the demand for proficient English speakers in professional settings continues to grow, the role of Business English instructors remains essential in shaping the future of global business communication.

11-2

Teaching Academic English

Academic English is a specialized form of the English language used in educational settings, primarily in higher education. It is essential for students to master academic English to succeed in their academic endeavors, as it is the language of instruction, research, and communication in most universities worldwide. In this comprehensive article, we will explore the significance of teaching academic English, strategies for effective instruction, and best practices to support learners in acquiring this crucial skill.

The Significance of Teaching Academic English

1. Facilitating Academic Success
Teaching academic English equips students with the language skills necessary to excel in their academic pursuits. It ensures that students can comprehend complex academic texts, participate in classroom discussions, and express their ideas clearly in written assignments and examinations.

2. Fostering Critical Thinking
Proficiency in academic English is closely linked to critical thinking skills. Through the process of engaging with academic texts, students

develop the ability to analyze, evaluate, and synthesize information effectively.

3. Promoting Global Competence

In an increasingly globalized world, proficiency in academic English enables students to participate in international academic communities and research collaborations. It enhances their ability to communicate and collaborate with peers and scholars from diverse linguistic backgrounds.

Strategies for Teaching Academic English

1. Integrated Language Instruction
Incorporate academic English instruction into the curriculum across disciplines, rather than treating it as a separate subject. Integrate language development activities into regular coursework to make the learning process more contextual and meaningful.

2. Vocabulary and Terminology
Explicitly teach discipline-specific vocabulary and terminology relevant to the students' field of study. Create glossaries, flashcards, and context-based exercises to help students build a strong academic vocabulary.

3. Reading Comprehension
Develop students' reading comprehension skills by providing them with challenging academic texts. Encourage close reading, annotation, and discussions to enhance understanding and critical analysis.

4. Writing Skills
Focus on developing students' writing skills by teaching them the conventions of academic writing, including proper citation, organization,

and argumentation. Provide feedback on drafts to help students improve their writing.

5. Speaking and Presentation Skills

Engage students in class discussions, debates, and presentations to develop their oral communication skills. Encourage them to articulate their ideas clearly and coherently.

6. Peer Feedback and Collaboration

Foster a supportive learning environment where students can provide peer feedback on each other's work. Collaborative learning activities can help students practice using academic language in context.

7. Technology and Multimedia Resources

Incorporate technology and multimedia resources, such as online databases, academic podcasts, and interactive simulations, to expose students to authentic academic content and language.

Best Practices for Teaching Academic English

1. Differentiated Instruction

Recognize that students may enter the classroom with varying levels of English proficiency. Differentiate instruction to meet individual learners' needs, providing additional support for those who require it.

2. Cultural Sensitivity

Be aware of the cultural backgrounds and experiences of your students, as this can affect their language learning. Create a culturally inclusive classroom that respects and values diverse perspectives.

3. Clear Learning Objectives

Set clear and achievable learning objectives for each lesson or unit, specifying the language skills and competencies students should develop.

4. Assessment and Feedback

Implement formative and summative assessments to gauge students' progress in academic English. Provide constructive feedback that helps students understand their strengths and areas for improvement.

5. Authentic Materials

Use authentic academic materials, such as research articles, scholarly papers, and conference presentations, to expose students to real-world language usage in their academic fields.

6. Scaffolding

Provide scaffolding support as students build their academic English skills. Start with simpler tasks and gradually increase the complexity of assignments to ensure students can apply what they've learned.

7. Professional Development

Stay informed about best practices in teaching academic English through professional development opportunities, workshops, and conferences. Continuously update your teaching strategies to meet evolving needs.

Teaching academic English is a critical component of preparing students for success in higher education and beyond. It fosters not only language proficiency but also critical thinking, communication, and global competence. By implementing effective strategies and best practices, educators can empower their students to navigate the complex world of academia with confidence and skill, ultimately opening doors to a wide range of academic and professional opportunities.

11-3

Teaching English for Specific Purposes (ESP)

Teaching English for Specific Purposes (ESP) is an approach to language education that has gained significant attention and relevance in recent years. Unlike general English language instruction, ESP is designed to meet the specific language needs of learners who require English for their professional or academic pursuits. This specialized form of language teaching is characterized by its focus on delivering targeted and practical language skills, vocabulary, and communication strategies, tailored to the specific demands of a particular field or discipline. This article provides an in-depth exploration of Teaching English for Specific Purposes, its principles, methodologies, and the advantages it offers to learners.

Defining ESP

ESP, as the name suggests, is all about specificity. It is an approach to language teaching that caters to learners who have a particular purpose for learning English, whether it be in the context of business, medicine, engineering, aviation, law, or any other specialized field. The central idea behind ESP is to equip learners with the linguistic tools and competencies necessary for effective communication and comprehension in their chosen professional or academic domain.

Key Principles of ESP

1. Needs Analysis: ESP instructors begin by conducting a thorough needs analysis. This process involves identifying the specific language skills, vocabulary, and communicative functions required by learners in their target context. The needs analysis is often done through surveys, interviews, or analysis of authentic texts used in the target field.
2. Targeted Content: ESP courses are designed to provide learners with content that is directly relevant to their area of specialization. This content includes specialized terminology, jargon, and discourse patterns that are commonly used in the target field. This ensures that learners acquire the language skills they need to perform effectively in their professional or academic roles.
3. Authentic Materials: ESP instructors rely heavily on authentic materials, such as industry reports, academic journals, technical manuals, and real-world documents. These materials expose learners to the language as it is used in their specific field, helping them develop the ability to understand and produce such texts.
4. Communicative Approach: ESP courses emphasize the development of practical communication skills. Learners are encouraged to engage in tasks and activities that simulate real-life communication situations they are likely to encounter in their professional or academic settings. This promotes meaningful language use and interaction.
5. Task-Based Learning: Task-based learning is a common pedagogical approach in ESP. Learners are given tasks or projects that mirror the tasks they will encounter in their profession. This not only reinforces language skills but also enhances problem-solving abilities and critical thinking.

Methodologies in ESP

ESP encompasses a wide range of methodologies, and the choice of methodology depends on various factors, including the learners' needs, the specific field of study, and the teaching context. Some of the common methodologies in ESP include:

1. Content-Based Instruction (CBI): In CBI, language instruction is integrated with content from the learners' field of study. This approach ensures that language learning is contextually relevant and meaningful.
2. Task-Based Language Teaching (TBLT): TBLT focuses on teaching language through tasks or activities that mirror real-world situations. Learners engage in tasks that require them to use the language in practical ways.
3. Simulation and Role-Play: These activities are used to recreate workplace or academic scenarios. Learners take on roles and engage in communication that mimics professional or academic interactions.
4. Needs-Based Instruction: This approach tailors the curriculum and materials to meet the specific needs of learners, identified through a needs analysis.
5. Genre Analysis: In this methodology, learners study the genres or types of texts commonly used in their field. They learn to recognize and produce these text types effectively.

Advantages of Teaching ESP

1. Relevance: ESP courses provide learners with skills and knowledge directly applicable to their chosen field, making the learning experience highly relevant and engaging.
2. Efficiency: Learners can acquire the necessary language skills more efficiently and quickly when they focus on the language they need for specific purposes.
3. Motivation: Learners are often highly motivated in ESP courses because they see the immediate practical value of what they are learning.

4. Improved Communication: ESP equips learners with the ability to communicate effectively in professional or academic settings, enhancing their career prospects and academic success.
5. Enhanced Confidence: As learners gain confidence in their language skills within their specific domain, they are better prepared to participate actively in their profession or academic field.
6. Adaptability: ESP is adaptable and can be tailored to suit the changing needs of learners as they progress in their careers or studies.

Challenges and Considerations

While ESP offers numerous advantages, it also comes with challenges and considerations:

1. Specialized Expertise: ESP instructors need to have a deep understanding of both language teaching methodologies and the specific field of study or profession they are teaching.
2. Resource Availability: Developing or sourcing authentic materials and resources for ESP can be challenging, particularly in less common or specialized fields.
3. Ongoing Needs Assessment: The specific language needs of learners may change over time, necessitating continuous needs assessment and curriculum adaptation.
4. Learner Diversity: ESP classes often consist of learners with varying levels of language proficiency and backgrounds, requiring differentiated instruction.

Teaching English for Specific Purposes (ESP) is a dynamic and highly effective approach to language education that caters to learners' specialized needs in professional or academic contexts. ESP courses are characterized by their tailored content, authentic materials, communicative focus, and task-based learning methods. By equipping learners with the language skills and competencies they need for their specific field, ESP empowers them to excel in their careers or academic pursuits, fostering enhanced communication, confidence, and adaptability. While ESP poses challenges such as the need for specialized expertise and ongoing needs assessment, its advantages make it an invaluable tool for language educators and learners alike in today's globalized world.

11-4

Teaching English to Young Learners

Teaching English to young learners can be a rewarding but challenging endeavor. Young learners, typically between the ages of 3 and 12, have unique needs, characteristics, and learning styles that require specialized teaching approaches. In this comprehensive article, we will explore the strategies, challenges, and best practices for teaching English to young learners.

Understanding Young Learners

Before delving into teaching strategies, it's essential to understand the cognitive, social, and emotional development of young learners. Young children are highly impressionable and absorb information like sponges. Their brains are rapidly developing, and they are curious by nature. Here are some key points to keep in mind:

1. **Cognitive Development:**
   - Young learners are in the process of acquiring their first language(s) and are naturally inclined to learn new languages.
   - They learn through play, exploration, and concrete experiences.
   - Their attention span is limited, so lessons should be short, engaging, and age-appropriate.

2. Social Development:
   - Young children are social beings and thrive in interactive and collaborative environments.
   - They may have varying levels of language proficiency, so differentiation is crucial.

3. Emotional Development:
   - Young learners often have limited control over their emotions, so creating a safe and nurturing classroom environment is essential.
   - They may experience frustration and anxiety when faced with language barriers.

Strategies for Teaching English to Young Learners

Effective teaching strategies for young learners should take into account their developmental stages and needs. Here are some strategies to consider:

1. Use Visuals and Props:
   - Young children are visual learners, so use flashcards, pictures, and real-life objects to illustrate vocabulary and concepts.
   - Incorporate colorful and age-appropriate visuals in teaching materials.

2. Songs and Chants:
   - Children love music and rhythm. Incorporate songs and chants to teach vocabulary and pronunciation.
   - Actions and gestures can enhance comprehension and engagement.

3. Games and Activities:
   - Incorporate games like bingo, memory matching, and board games to make learning fun.

- Use activities that promote physical movement, such as Simon says or role-playing.

4. Storytelling:
    - Young learners enjoy listening to stories. Use age-appropriate picture books and create interactive storytelling sessions.
    - Encourage them to retell stories in their own words to develop speaking skills.

5. Total Physical Response (TPR):
    - TPR involves associating language with physical actions. This can help young learners understand and remember vocabulary.
    - For instance, you can teach "jump" by having students physically jump.

6. Repetition and Routine:
    - Young learners benefit from repetition and routine. Revisit and reinforce previously learned material in each lesson.
    - Establish a predictable daily or weekly routine to create a sense of security.

7. Communication and Interaction:
    - Create opportunities for young learners to communicate in English through pair and group activities.
    - Encourage them to ask questions and express themselves, even if their language skills are limited.

8. Cultural Sensitivity:
    - Be sensitive to cultural differences and avoid stereotypes when teaching about different cultures and countries where English is spoken.

Challenges in Teaching English to Young Learners

Teaching English to young learners is not without its challenges. Here are some common difficulties teachers may encounter and how to address them:

1. Attention Span:
- Young learners have short attention spans, so keep lessons brief and engaging.
- Use a variety of activities to maintain their interest.

2. Different Levels:
- In a classroom of young learners, there can be a wide range of language proficiency levels.
- Differentiate instruction by providing additional support for struggling students and challenging activities for more advanced learners.

3. Classroom Management:
- Managing young learners in a classroom can be challenging due to their energy levels and potential behavioral issues.
- Establish clear rules and routines, and use positive reinforcement techniques.

4. Limited Vocabulary:
- Young learners may have a limited vocabulary in their first language, which can make it challenging to introduce new concepts.
- Build on their existing knowledge and use visuals to aid comprehension.

5. Assessment:
- Traditional testing methods may not be suitable for young learners.
- Use alternative assessment methods like observation, portfolios, and checklists to gauge their progress.

Best Practices for Teaching English to Young Learners

To ensure success in teaching English to young learners, consider these best practices:

1. Create a Positive Learning Environment:
- Foster a welcoming and safe classroom environment where children feel valued and comfortable expressing themselves.

2. Be Patient and Flexible:
- Young learners may require extra time to grasp concepts, so be patient and adapt your teaching methods as needed.

3. Communicate with Parents:
- Maintain open communication with parents to keep them informed about their child's progress and to involve them in their learning journey.

4. Professional Development:
- Stay up-to-date with the latest research, teaching methods, and resources for teaching young learners through ongoing professional development.

5. Reflect and Adapt:
- Regularly reflect on your teaching practices and make adjustments based on the needs and progress of your students.

6. Collaborate with Colleagues:
- Share ideas and collaborate with fellow teachers who have experience in teaching young learners to exchange strategies and resources.

7. Keep It Fun:
    - Remember that young learners thrive in a fun and engaging learning environment. Incorporate play and creativity into your lessons.

Teaching English to young learners is a challenging yet fulfilling endeavor. By understanding their developmental stages, employing effective strategies, and being aware of common challenges, teachers can create a positive and enriching language-learning experience for their students. With patience, creativity, and dedication, educators can instill a love for English in young learners that will benefit them throughout their lives.

Teaching English on a One-on-One Basis

Teaching English on a one-on-one basis, often referred to as "1-to-1" teaching, is a highly effective and personalized approach to language instruction. It allows educators to tailor their lessons to the specific needs and goals of individual learners, creating an environment where the student's progress can be accelerated. In this article, we will explore the benefits of one-on-one English teaching, strategies for effective instruction, and tips for both teachers and learners to make the most of this unique learning experience.

The Advantages of 1-to-1 English Teaching

1. Personalized Learning: One of the most significant advantages of one-on-one English teaching is the opportunity to customize the curriculum to suit the student's specific needs, goals, and learning style. This personalization leads to more rapid and meaningful progress.
2. Individual Attention: With one student and one teacher, there are no distractions or competition for the instructor's attention. This enables the teacher to focus on the student's weaknesses, adapt to their strengths, and provide instant feedback.

3. Faster Progress: Due to the tailored nature of one-on-one instruction, students often make faster progress in their language learning journey. Lessons can be adjusted according to the learner's pace, leading to efficient learning.
4. Improved Confidence: Individual learners often experience an increase in confidence as they receive individualized attention and witness steady improvements in their language skills. This boost in self-esteem is crucial for language acquisition.
5. Flexibility: One-on-one lessons allow for flexible scheduling and content. Students and teachers can work together to design a learning plan that fits the student's lifestyle and objectives.

Strategies for Effective One-on-One English Teaching

1. Needs Assessment: Begin by assessing the learner's needs, goals, and current language proficiency. This information serves as the foundation for creating a tailored curriculum.
2. Individualized Lesson Plans: Design lesson plans that cater to the student's unique requirements. This may include focusing on specific skills such as speaking, listening, reading, or writing, or targeting particular topics and vocabulary relevant to the learner's interests or profession.
3. Clear Objectives: Establish clear and achievable learning objectives for each lesson. Discuss these objectives with the student to ensure alignment and motivation.
4. Active Engagement: Encourage the student to actively participate in lessons. Engage in interactive activities, discussions, and real-world language tasks to make learning more dynamic and enjoyable.
5. Constructive Feedback: Provide timely and constructive feedback. Correct errors gently and encourage the student to learn from their mistakes. Positive reinforcement is essential for motivation.

6. Continuous Assessment: Regularly assess the student's progress to adjust the lesson plan as needed. This ensures that the instruction remains relevant and effective.
7. Encourage Autonomy: Foster independent learning by equipping the student with resources and strategies for self-study. This will empower them to continue improving outside of the one-on-one sessions.

Tips for Teachers

1. Patience and Empathy: Be patient with your students and empathetic to their struggles. Understand that everyone learns at their own pace.
2. Adaptability: Be ready to adapt your teaching methods and materials based on your student's progress and feedback.
3. Effective Communication: Ensure that you maintain open and clear communication with your student. Listen to their concerns, questions, and preferences.
4. Set Realistic Goals: Help your student set achievable language learning goals and provide guidance on how to reach them.
5. Professional Development: Continue to enhance your teaching skills by attending workshops, courses, and staying updated with the latest language teaching methodologies.

Tips for Learners

1. Communicate Your Goals: Be clear about your language learning objectives and preferred learning style. This will help your teacher create a customized plan.
2. Consistent Practice: Engage in regular language practice outside of lessons. Consistency is key to language acquisition.
3. Be Open to Feedback: Embrace constructive criticism and view it as an opportunity for growth. Mistakes are part of the learning process.

4. Self-Motivation: Take ownership of your learning journey and stay motivated. Set mini-goals to track your progress and celebrate achievements.

One-on-one English teaching is a highly effective approach to language instruction. The tailored nature of these lessons allows for personalized learning, individual attention, faster progress, and increased confidence. By following strategies for effective instruction, teachers can make the most of this method, while learners can maximize their language acquisition experience.

The journey of learning a new language is both challenging and rewarding. With one-on-one English teaching, the path becomes more efficient and enjoyable, ultimately leading to fluency and a broader world of opportunities.

www.ingramcontent.com/pod-product-compliance
Lightning Source LLC
LaVergne TN
LVHW011929070526
838202LV00054B/4552